"Practical, gentle, and thorough, this bc [ ] into your body and your senses. As you learn how to turn down the volume of the chatter and self-judgment there is more room to experience yourself as a whole, physical human being. What a relief, and what an opportunity! Highly recommended."

—**Steven C. Hayes, PhD**, cofounder of acceptance and commitment therapy (ACT) and author of *Get Out of Your Mind and Into Your Life*

"We humans are so often at war with our own bodies. We use our powerful intellect to break ourselves into parts—thighs, buttocks, stomach, nose—and then often judge these parts as 'not good enough.' We then waste energy trying to fix ourselves and/or become self-conscious and withdraw from life. *Living with Your body and Other Things You Hate* will help you to declare peace on your body, connect with it, nurture it, and appreciate it. The book never preaches. It uses practical exercises to take you on a gentle, mindful journey. If you are the sort of person who is hard on yourself and insecure about your body, then I believe this book will help you to accept yourself, find your inner strength, and build a life filled with joy and meaning."

—**Joseph Ciarrochi**, author of *Get out of Your Mind and Into Your Life for Teens* and *Mindfulness, Acceptance, and Positive Psychology*

"Full of wisdom and compassion, this is a beautifully written and highly practical guide to self-acceptance. I wish I'd read it thirty years ago; it would have saved me decades of self-loathing!"

—**Russ Harris**, author of *The Happiness Trap*

"If you are unhappy with your appearance in any way, this book will help you and others understand what you experience and why. It will explain why your feelings are devastating, and how your struggles to overcome it may have been futile. The authors provide a totally different way to approach the problem of poor self-image. If all other methods have failed, this book offers hope and guidance in a distinctly new way. Acceptance and commitment therapy techniques will teach you to live the life you want, follow your values, and stop struggling for an ideal image. The authors write in a very friendly manner, sharing their own experiences at times, and provide wonderful exercises to follow. I highly recommend this book to everyone who wants to stop struggling and begin living."

—**Fugen Neziroglu, PhD, ABBP, ABPP**, author of *Overcoming Body Dysmorphic Disorder* and *Body Dysmorphic Disorder: A Treatment Manual*

LIVING
with BODY
your
& Other Things
you HATE

How to Let Go of Your Struggle
with **BODY IMAGE** Using
Acceptance & Commitment Therapy

EMILY K. SANDOZ, PhD
TROY DuFRENE

New Harbinger Publications, Inc.

Publisher's Note

Distributed in Canada by Raincoast Books

Copyright © 2013 by Emily Sandoz and Troy DuFrene
New Harbinger Publications, Inc.
5674 Shattuck Avenue
Oakland, CA 94609
www.newharbinger.com

Cover design by Amy Shoup
Acquired by Catharine Meyers

Library of Congress Cataloging-in-Publication Data

Sandoz, Emily K.
  Living with your body and other things you hate : how to let go of your struggle with body image using acceptance and commitment therapy / Emily K. Sandoz, Troy DuFrene.
      pages cm
  Summary: "Are you comfortable with the skin you're in? If not, you aren't alone. Most people are dissatisfied with some aspect of their physical appearance, but if your unhappiness with your looks starts to take over your life, it's time to make a change. This book applies powerful acceptance and commitment therapy (ACT) principles to help you accept both your body and negative thoughts, and discover new feelings of validity beyond your reflection in the mirror"-- Provided by publisher.
  Includes bibliographical references.
  ISBN 978-1-60882-104-4 (pbk.) -- ISBN 978-1-60882-105-1 (pdf e-book) -- ISBN 978-1-60882-106-8 (epub) 1. Body image. 2. Self-esteem. 3. Acceptance and commitment therapy. I. DuFrene, Troy, 1972- II. Title.
  BF697.5.B63S36 2014
  306.4'613--dc23
                                        2013039164

Printed in the United States of America

15   14   13

10   9   8   7   6   5   4   3   2   1

First printing

To my mother, Anne, who taught me with such care the myriad ways a person can be beautiful

Contents

Part 1:

INTRODUCTION:

AN INVITATION

Ten minutes before the school bus was due, the young mother realized that her eight-year-old daughter, Hannah, was no longer at the breakfast table. "Hannah?" She called for the child several times as she buckled the baby into his carrier and pulled the coats from the closet. Hannah loved riding the bus. "You're going to miss it, sweetheart," she said as she pushed the bedroom door open. The young mother stopped in the doorway. Hannah, dressed in a blue sweater, stood staring into a full-length mirror, the favorite pink shirt she'd worn at the table bunched on the floor next to her. She turned and walked toward the doorway.

"It didn't look good, Momma," the child said, as she slipped her arms one by one into the coat her mother was holding. "I looked fat in the pink one."

As the day continued, the young mother found herself overwhelmed by the experience—first, by the urge to save her daughter from these concerns, then by the urge to understand them. What was it that caused the child to abandon her oatmeal that morning to check her appearance? What did she look for as she peered into the mirror? What did she see on her tiny eight-year-old body that she found unacceptable? Did she find relief in hiding what she saw under the thick sweater? How long before that relief would fade? How long before she would find herself peering into the mirror again? What else might she be willing to do to feel satisfied with what she saw there?

Where You Find Yourself

We're going to go ahead and assume that you find your eyes on these words right now because you know something about the experience of that little girl. Maybe you've slipped away from your own life at times to inspect your waist, your hips, your hair, or your skin. Maybe you know the familiar sinking feeling as your eyes come to rest on that part of your body you can't stand. You might recognize the need to continue peering at your reflection, fixing (or fantasizing about fixing) what you see, even if looking at yourself disgusts or depresses you. You might recognize the relief that comes when you feel okay with what you see in the mirror.

For some of you, perhaps this hasn't been a very serious problem. Maybe you recognize that you worry a lot about how you look, but it's never really gotten in the way of any of your relationships, your work, your health, or anything else that matters to you. But then again, maybe it has. We're writing this book right now because for many people, body image is a problem.

Millions of people will organize whole chunks of their lives today around how they feel about the way they look. They'll wake up an hour early to style their hair or apply their makeup. They'll change out of a shirt they love because it doesn't look like they think it should, or they'll skip lunch with a friend so they can fit in another workout. Some will pretend to be sick so no one wonders why they aren't eating, and others will avoid the eyes of someone who cares about them so they don't have to imagine what she might see.

It's not that there's anything wrong with choosing to change clothes or skip lunch or hold back in a conversation. It's when a person can't choose, or even see the choice, that the problems begin. Millions of people today will live their lives to manage their feelings about their bodies, not because they want to, but because they really can't see another way to be right now.

It's a funny thing, choice. Folks have made careers as intellectuals for thousands of years arguing about whether or not choice exists. Are the things we do determined, or do we have freedom to choose our actions? Don't worry. We're not going to make an intellectual argument here for or against free will. No matter your beliefs on such things; we're not particularly interested in whether or not choice *really* exists. What we are interested in is the *experience* of choice, the *experience* of freedom.

Let's pause here for a moment to explore a little bit about what we mean. Call to mind a moment when you felt really free—not burdened or pushed or squeezed down—just there, where you were. It might be something recent, or you might have to reach way back in your memory to find that free moment. It might be something really important to your life—a big day that others would remember. Or it might be something simple, like a smell that reminds you of spring or of your grandmother. What you're looking for here is any free moment. A moment you would choose.

We're serious, by the way. We are actually asking you to do this. Right now. In fact, you might want to get into the habit of grabbing a notebook or opening a blank note on your smartphone each time you pick up this book. Throughout the book, we'll invite you to notice your thoughts, feelings, or memories and write down what you notice. Other times, something will strike you as worth making a note of. We hope you use our little book in this way.

See, the thing about this sort of book is that just reading about things that you *could* do differently is not likely to result in much change. Our guess is that you're holding this book in your hand because you've thought about ways that your life could be different and things you could do differently. This book is designed to help you shift from thinking into doing, but it's going to depend on you. We invite you to stop reading for a moment, to let go of analyzing or figuring things out. Take a deep breath and try this out:

Call to mind a moment of freedom in your life. Close your eyes and take five slow, deep breaths, as if you could breathe that moment in, letting it fill you up from the inside out.

Got one? If not, go back, close your eyes, take a deep breath and see if you can't open up to the memory of a free moment in your life. Don't worry too much about picking the perfect moment. Just let your mind arrive at any moment in which you felt free and pause there for a while.

Now, without letting that sense of freedom pass from you, imagine you could fill your life with moments like this—with moments you have deliberately chosen. Imagine you could string a bunch of those free moments together to build your life journey. Is this something you'd want? Something you'd be willing to work for? Take a moment to imagine what that might be like. If you have thoughts like, *That's unlikely* or *That would be hard* or *Maybe I don't really care about freedom*, just notice those thoughts and how hard it is to imagine something more.

And now, whenever you're ready, we invite you to stop reading once more, to take a slow deep breath, and to call to mind a moment of restriction, a moment when you felt trapped.

Call to mind a moment when you found yourself really stuck. Close your eyes and really see yourself in that moment. Take five slow, deep breaths, as if you could breathe that moment in, letting it fill you up from the inside out.

Did you get one? You might have found it's a little bit harder to open up to one of those. You might find yourself wanting to skip ahead a little at this point. Remember, these are just invitations. And... we wonder if inviting difficult stuff to show up is part of what helps us to move through it.

So, if you were willing to hang out in a stuck moment for five breaths, what did you notice? How much life was in this moment? How much room to breathe? What thoughts and feelings showed up as you called a stuck moment to mind? Are moments like this something you've worked to avoid? Will it be a relief to move on to the next paragraph?

Notice that in just those few moments, just in the time it took to take ten breaths, you were able to experience freedom and restriction. Without anything in the world changing, you moved from a moment of freedom to a moment of restriction. And we're not just talking about the kinds of thoughts and feelings that showed up there. We're not talking about hard thoughts and easy thoughts or the difference between joy and pain. You could just as easily call to mind a moment of freedom in which you were experiencing great pain in the form of disappointment or regret. In fact, you may have felt a kernel of hurt right inside the moment of freedom you called up already.

The thing is, there doesn't seem to be much of a relationship between the experience of freedom and actual freedom. You wouldn't have to think very long to call to mind folks who had the resources to do pretty much anything they pleased and still found themselves trapped inside their drinking, or their dieting, or their work, or their attempts to be someone else. We've also all known folks who had extraordinarily few of their needs met and were still able to live freely.

See, it doesn't seem to matter if your childhood, or your genetics, or a supreme being, or the position of the stars made that moment of freedom more likely. It seems like people can find freedom, can find meaning and purpose, right inside the lives that they already have.

We are writing this book because we care about people finding freedom in their lives and because we've known far too many people who found themselves trapped in a struggle with their own bodies. If you know something about that struggle, and if you are ready for something different, welcome.

What's Led You Here?

So how is it that you came to be reading about our hopes for your freedom? We're guessing that this is not the first time you've thought about wanting to do something about your struggle with the way you look. We're also guessing that our little book is not the first thing you've tried. There are tons of things that are easier than snagging a self-help book off the shelf, and our guess is that you've tried a number of them.

If you're like most of our readers, you could list a number of things you've done to try to get rid of body image problems. Go ahead and let your mind roll over a few of them. What do you do when you notice your struggle with your body?

Most of the things folks do fall into one of two categories: changing the way they look, or changing the way they feel about the way they look. In your case, maybe you've tried to distract yourself or to push thoughts about your appearance out of your mind. Maybe you've tried to convince yourself to let it go, that you shouldn't worry so much about the way you look. Maybe you've made efforts to hide your flaws. Maybe you've tried medications, diets, surgeries, or exercise programs. Maybe it feels like if you could just fix your appearance once and for all, you could finally get on with living your life. Take a moment and notice the mental and emotional effort you've put into this.

And maybe, just maybe, you're thinking that buried deep inside this book is the answer you've been looking for, the one thing you haven't tried, the ultimate source of relief from all those terrible thoughts and feelings you have about your body.

If this were your typical psychology self-help book, we might share that thought. We'd start off by telling you about how body image develops and how it can go sideways. We might ask you to notice where you learned to judge your body and to respond to those judgments. Then we'd hustle you into different ways to improve that body image. We might encourage you to look at how you talk to yourself about your body and where that self-talk came from. We might teach you relaxation exercises to use when the tension becomes overwhelming. We might advise you to focus on the features you love about yourself or to remind yourself of the things that are more important than appearance. We might teach you new ways to try to enjoy your body. We'd offer you this to try and that to try. We'd give you brand-new tips and fancy tricks that would help you to work at that same job you've been at since you were the little kid in the mirror—trying to like how you look.

And while you're working hard at liking your appearance, where's your life heading? How are you reaching out for your values? Where's the freedom you've known and maybe still long for? For most the idea goes something like this: *If I could just look in the mirror without hating what I see, I could finally go after that life I want.* You could get that job. Or take that class. Or have that talk. Maybe you're hoping that buried somewhere in chapter 7 is the tip that's going to release you from feeling bad about your body so you can finally get on with your life.

We should go ahead and confess: this book is not about changing how you feel about your body any more than it is full of tips on how to look good. It's worth saying again: we're not going to teach you to like your body. We don't think you need any more of that kind of advice. In fact, we think that if strategies for feeling better or looking better were going to help you live your life, you wouldn't be reading this book. We wonder if there isn't another way to let go of this struggle—a way that doesn't depend on changing how you look or even how you feel about how you look.

So how about it?

What we're talking about here isn't for everyone. It involves letting go of a lot of what you know about how things work and about how you yourself work. Here's how you know if this book is for you: Are you tired of letting this struggle fill more and more of your life? Are you finding yourself further and further from the life you used to dream of? Most importantly, are you ready to try something different, even if you're not sure exactly what that looks like?

Where You Could Be Headed

Truth is, we wonder if the world all around you isn't filled with opportunities to live the life you would dream of. Not necessarily the life your mother (or your brother, or your partner, or your second-grade teacher) would want for you. Not even the life that we might pick for you. We are explicitly interested in the life *you* would choose, the one you would reach out and pluck from all the possibilities. The life that you would value, the life that you would work for. The life in which you could find your freedom.

Think about the way you move about your life. Start with just the past day. In the past twenty-four hours, how many moves have you made that were about something that really matters to you? How many actions have you taken that brought you closer to the person that you want to be? If you're like most people, the answer is somewhere between "Uh... not many" and "I have no earthly idea." The fact of the matter is that we don't tend to think about such things too often. We can get through much of our lives in a fairly productive way without it being very meaningful at all. In some cases, we can get through much of our lives without even being there.

It's sort of like this. Imagine you awaken suddenly in the middle of an unfamiliar forest. You blink a couple of times, stretch, and start to look around. You spend a moment taking it all in, when suddenly you hear a creepy growl coming from your left. So you look quickly toward the noise, do a quick scan to locate a path in the other direction, jump up, and start running. Imagine that you run and run, dodging branches, hopping over ditches, and every glance behind you confirms that something is hot on your trail.

As you run, are you likely to notice a lovely fragrance? A gentle breeze? Are you likely to stop and appreciate the way the sun filters through the trees around you or the warmth it brings to your skin? For most of us, the answer is no. When we are running from something, we pay attention to two things: the thing that means danger and the thing that means our escape.

The problem is, of course, that we humans spend so much of our lives running from something. We start early, like that little girl changing her clothes to get away from feeling fat. We run from fears, from memories, from doubts, from regret, from sadness, from disgust. We run by keeping to ourselves or by avoiding being alone, by zoning out or by homing in on one thing, by working too hard or by holding back any real effort. We run by trying to change how we look and by trying to change how we feel about how we look. We run and run. Each of us runs from our own danger in our own way. And as we run, we miss out on our own lives. We miss out on the opportunities to live the life that matters to us.

What if working through this book could help you to pause just long enough to see opportunities in your own life? What if working through this book could help you to slow down enough to choose your own direction? What if working through this book is the first step in building the life you value?

Who We Are

Considering that we're asking you to step into something different with us, to face your most private struggles and most important desires, it makes sense to us to tell you a little bit about ourselves. Emily is an assistant professor in the department of psychology of University of Louisiana at Lafayette. She also works as a therapist using *acceptance and commitment therapy* (or ACT, which is said like a word and not letters), the treatment approach on which this book is based. Emily's been interested in body image for some time. Having spent much of her adolescence on the stage or looking in the mirror preparing for the stage, Emily left high school with a sense of how important what we see in the mirror can seem and how terribly it can disrupt our lives. Emily started out doing research and writing about how struggling with the body can result in eating problems. She soon recognized, however, that body struggles end up taking meaning from folks' lives in all sorts of ways. Hating the body isn't always about fat and managing that hatred isn't always about eating or not eating. She started taking her research in another direction. And just as they were finishing up their last book on disordered eating, *The Mindfulness and Acceptance Workbook for Bulimia*, Emily contacted Troy about writing this book—a book she hoped could reach out more broadly to all the people who, just like you, are finding the struggle with body image to be taking over their lives.

Troy is a writer who stumbled upon Emily and ACT in 2007 while doing research for a self-help book he was writing. They partnered up in a workshop, Emily made Troy cry, and they ended up working together with her mentor, Kelly Wilson, on several writing projects. Troy didn't particularly like how it felt when Emily first started talking about how we all struggle with our bodies. But he knew there weren't many places where people could admit to such things, let alone try something different, so when Emily asked Troy to help with this book, he answered with a resounding yes.

Perhaps as important to our work here as who we are, how we met, or any training we've had is that we, Emily and Troy, both live inside of bodies that we don't always like a whole lot. In fact, we've both had stretches in which we spent more time hating our bodies—and struggling with that hate—than we did living our lives. We are people who know what it's like to be trapped inside of our own skin, and we are people who care about finding freedom.

The Invitation

Now that you have some sense of who we are and of where we think we might head next, we extend to you an invitation to come along. The strange thing about this invitation is that we don't have any idea what the steps are between here and the life you want. We're inviting you along on this journey, not as our companion, but as the leader on your own path. Only you can see and feel the obstacles in front of you. Only you can choose the life that you want to live. Using the tools we'll set out for you in this book, you'll discover your unique path around the barriers you confront. Along the way, your job will be to notice the obstacles and opportunities and choose how to move through them, while we'll be offering invitations and techniques to help you do so.

We can't know for sure what it will be like for you, but we can pretty safely assume that it's going to be as hard as it is useful. That being said, there are ways to make it pretty easy. You could hold back from applying this to anything that really matters in your life. Keep it distant. Play it safe. The problem is, of course, that it's probably not worth doing if it can't really matter to you.

So we invite you to take a risk. Not just any risk: we invite you to risk feeling uncomfortable, disappointed, disgusted, and frustrated. Not because we think you might feel that way as you work through the book, but because we *assume* you *will* feel that way at some point. But not for nothing. We invite you to risk thinking and feeling all the unpleasant things that come up around your body for a purpose.

What would you be willing to experience when you look in the mirror if it meant you got to live more freely?

What if you could build a meaningful life without having to change your body or the pain it brings?

We invite you to come along and find out.

1 Your Body Image

The first thing to do when charting a course for any journey is to figure out exactly where you are. After all, it's hard to know which step to take if you're not sure where you're standing. In this section we're going to take a look at body image difficulties: what they are, how they are learned, and how they come to interfere with people's lives. In some books, this would involve us telling you what we know about how body image works and you figuring out whether or not you think we're right. This is not that kind of book. See, we don't think that what we know about these difficulties from studies, working with clients, or our own struggles is enough to tell you where you are. So we're going to take a look at how your body image difficulties work (and don't work) for you.

What Is "Body Image"?

First let's clear up what we even mean by "body image." Often when folks say "body image" out in the world, they mean issues or problems with the body. When psychologists and other professionals use the term "body image," they mean simply how the body is experienced. Everyone has a body image. It's not a term that means that something is broken or somebody is messed up.

And even though "image" sounds like something you imagine, something tucked away in your mind somewhere, we use the term "body image" to mean somebody's whole experience of his or her body (Cash 2008). Body image includes the feeling of your clothes on your skin, the grumbling in your stomach, or an ache in your head. It includes the shape of your stomach or hips, the tone of your muscles, the color of your skin, and the way your hair frames your face. Body image includes how your body feels from the inside out and how it looks from the outside in. It also includes how you think and feel about those experiences.

Noticing Your Body Image

In just a moment, we are going to invite you to take some time to notice each of these aspects of your body experience. We're going to go ahead and warn you that this probably won't be easy. If your body image was easy for you, you wouldn't be reading this book. We think, though, that getting a good sense of *how* it's not easy is one of the first steps of this work. If you have some sense that there could be value in this for you, we invite you to set aside some time to move through the exercises that make up the rest of this chapter.

If you notice yourself struggling with thoughts like *I should really do this* or *I don't really have a choice at this point*, see if you can't let go of that struggle. If bullying yourself was going to work, it probably would have already. Instead, imagine that you could give this time to yourself as a gift. See if you can't offer up this work as a way of honoring yourself. And any time you need a break, set this work down until you are willing to pick it up again.

From the Inside Out

One aspect of your body image is the way you feel inside your skin. Most folks who struggle with body image will note that they pay attention to few sensations in their bodies, if any. Now, if you're willing, take a moment to notice your body image from the inside out. Don't forget to have paper or a blank document ready so you can write down what you notice. Audio files for this practice and other practices in this book are available for download at www .newharbinger.com/21044. The audio for this practice is called track 1. See the back of the book for more information about how to download the audio tracks.

PRACTICE: Noticing Body Image, Part One–From the Inside Out

Take a breath and let your eyes fall gently closed. As your eyes come closed, take a moment to notice what it feels like to breathe, the gentle in and out of your breath.

When you have a sense of the gentle rhythm of your breath in your body, let your attention slip down into the very tips of your toes, then slowly work its way up your body from the very tips of your toes to the very top of your head, shifting slowly from one body area to the next with each breath.

One full breath for your toes. In. And out.

One full breath for the soles of your feet. In. And out.

And when you find yourself losing track of what it is you were doing, just gently return your attention to your breath.

Now, one full breath for your ankles.

And one full breath for your shins.
Take one full breath for your knees.
Now, one full breath for your thighs.
And one full breath for your bottom.
Take one full breath for your belly.
Now, one full breath for your sternum.
Take one full breath for your neck and shoulders.
And one full breath for your upper arms.
Now, one full breath for your elbows.
Take one full breath for your wrists.
And now going back, take one full breath for your throat.
Now, one full breath for your chin.
Take one full breath for your nose and eyes.
And take one full breath for your forehead.
And finally, one full breath for the top of your head.
And, when you're ready, take one last deep breath and let it out slowly. And, when you're ready, allow your awareness to come back to the room around you.

So what kinds of things did you notice? Take a moment and jot down some of the things that showed up for you as you paid attention to your body experience in this way. A couple of tips before you start writing: Try to be as specific as you can. For example, if you start to write "my feet," you might write, "the way these shoes squeeze my little toe, the heat and pressure I feel there." If you find yourself reaching to remember what you noticed, it may be worth stopping to take a deep breath and dip briefly back into that eyes-closed observation. You'll be surprised at how quickly you can call things up. They don't have to be related to the instructions in the exercise. They can be something totally unrelated, in fact. Just record anything you noticed.

Take a look over the things that you wrote down. This list might be mostly tactile sensations like pressure, pain, or temperature. Notice, though, what else is there—what else, if anything, you noticed.

16

From the Outside In

Now, if you're willing, we'll take a few moments to notice your body image in a different way: from the outside in. If you're like most folks who struggle with body image, you have a complex relationship with your reflection. On the one hand, it's probably painful to be faced with your appearance. You may find yourself unable to look in the mirror without feeling upset and trying different things to fix what you see. On the other hand, going without seeing yourself, without having the opportunity to fix your appearance, may feel much worse. This may mean that you spend more time than you would like to in front of the mirror and more time than you would like avoiding your reflection.

And that's exactly why this is probably a good place to pause to get a sense of your body image. We're not going to ask you to jump in front of a mirror just yet. We are, however, going to ask you to call your appearance to mind, and to take a few moments to pay attention to how you see your body. If you're using the audio tracks, go to track 2 now.

PRACTICE: Noticing Body Image, Part Two–From the Outside In

Once more, start with a deep breath and let your eyes come closed, taking a few moments to notice what it feels like to breathe, and letting that feeling of breathing settle you in.

Imagine yourself before a full-length mirror exactly as you are right now, as if you suddenly noticed a mirror across from you and stood up to consider your reflection.

On your next breath, imagine that you were to rest your eyes upon the reflection of your feet and gradually move your eyes up your body, slowly taking in your appearance, letting your breath pace you.

17

Imagine that you were studying your body, seeking to memorize every detail.

One full breath for your toes. In. And out.

One full breath for the soles of your feet. In. And out.

And when you find yourself losing track of what it is you were doing, just gently return your attention to your breath, then to the next area of your body.

And when you find yourself wanting to stop and go on, see if you can't stay with yourself just a moment longer, in this hard place.

Now, one full breath for your ankles.

And one full breath for your shins.

Take one full breath for your knees.

Now, one full breath for your thighs.

And now just take one breath to center yourself again. And let it out slowly.

Now take one full breath for your belly.

Now, one full breath for your sternum

Take one full breath for your neck and shoulders.

And one full breath for your upper arms.

Now, one full breath for your elbows.

Take one full breath for your wrists.

And now going back, take one full breath for your throat.

Now, one full breath for your chin.

Take one full breath for your nose and eyes.

And take one full breath for your forehead.

And finally, one full breath for the top of your head.

And, when you're ready, take one last deep breath and let it out slowly. And, when you're ready, allow your awareness to come back to the room around you.

What kinds of things did you notice? Take a moment to write down some of the things that showed up for you as you paid attention to your body experience in this way. Remember to note specific details of the things that entered your attention, even if they seem unrelated. And again, if you find yourself reaching to remember what you noticed, it may be worth closing your eyes and taking a slow, deep breath before letting the rest of your image fill in.

Take a look over the things that you wrote down. This list might be mostly visual sensations: colors, shadows, and shapes. Notice, though, what else is there—what else, if anything, you noticed.

Now take a look at both of your lists together. Did you write down anything besides the things you saw with your eyes or felt in your body? How about the things you didn't write down? Take a moment to notice the other things that came up for you as you experienced your body.

Now, if you're willing, pick some experience of your body that was difficult for you to spend time noticing—maybe even too difficult to put words around. Was there anything else that you experienced as you noticed that part of your body you wish you could fix? Was there anything else that came up as you noticed the sensations in your body you'd do anything to get rid of?

Thoughts and Feelings

We said earlier that much of your body image is made up of how your body feels from the inside out and how it looks from the outside in. That's not all, though. See, one amazing thing about we humans is that our experience in any one moment is not limited by the world happening all around us. We not only see and hear and taste and smell and touch, we also wonder and remember and consider and hope and regret. Your body image is not only what you see with your eyes or feel in your body. It includes the thoughts and feelings that rise up around your body. If you're willing now, take a moment to notice body image again, this time noticing the thoughts and feelings tucked right inside of your perceptual experience. If you're using the audio tracks, go to track 3 now.

PRACTICE: Noticing Body Image, Part Three–Thoughts and Feelings

Take a deep breath and let your eyes come closed. Feel the gentle in and out of your breath.

Imagine yourself once more before a full-length mirror. Take a few breaths here, considering your reflection as you carry it with you in your mind. Notice any thoughts that come up and the feelings they carry with them. These might be judgments or memories or other images.

Next, imagine scanning your body again, from the tips of your toes up to the very top of your head, this time paying special attention not only to the image before you, but to any thoughts and feelings that come up around that image.

One full breath for your toes. In. And out.

What else shows up when you notice your toes? In. And out.

One full breath for the soles of your feet. In. And out.

What else shows up when you notice your feet? In. And out.

And when you find yourself losing track of what it is you were doing, just gently return your attention to your breath.

And when you find yourself wanting to stop or skip on to the next thing, see if you can't stay with yourself just a moment longer, in this hard place.

And when you find yourself losing track of what it is you were doing, just gently return your attention to your breath.

Now, one full breath for your ankles.

And one full breath for your shins.

Take one full breath for your knees.

Now, one full breath for your thighs.

And now take one long, slow, deep breath to center yourself. And let it out slowly.

And then take one full breath for your belly.

Now, one full breath for your sternum.

Take one full breath for your neck and shoulders.
And one full breath for your upper arms.
Now, one full breath for your elbows.
Take one full breath for your wrists.
And now going back, take one full breath for your throat.
Now, one full breath for your chin.
Take one full breath for your nose and eyes.
And take one full breath for your forehead.
And finally, one full breath for the top of your head.
And, when you're ready, take one last deep breath and let it out slowly. And, when you're ready, allow your awareness to come back to the room around you.

What showed up for you this time? Take a moment and write down the thoughts and feelings that showed up for you as you paid attention to your body experience in this way. Note the details as they come to you, pausing to call your experience up again if you find yourself struggling for the memory.

Take a moment to read over the things that you wrote down. You may notice that some of these seem like new thoughts or feelings you may have never even noticed you have. Others will be old and familiar thoughts and feelings that come up anytime things get rough between you and your body. Notice which of these came up in earlier exercises, as you experienced your body from the outside in or inside out.

Now, look at your three lists together. Notice the things you wrote and the things you didn't write. Take your time reading over these experiences. Notice any urges to hurry through, or skip to the next chapter, or put the book aside. See if you can't take some time to bear witness to the ways you experience your body and the ways you struggle with that experience. In this next section, we'll talk about how people come to struggle with body image, but we're not really interested in how this works for people *in general*. And we're not convinced that that would be particularly helpful for you. Instead, we want you to relate the way body image works for most people to the way it works for *you*.

Struggling with Body Image

Everyone has a body image. In fact, the body experience is an important part of human functioning. Being able to sense what's going on in our bodies helps to keep us safe and healthy. Being able to sense where our bodies are in space allows us to dance and run and move the way we want to. Being able to recognize ourselves and change the way we look gives us a way to express who we are. But that's not all.

Body image can also become a problem in our lives. Being able to feel our clothes pressing against our bodies helps us to evaluate when our bodies are bigger than we want them to be. Being able to recognize ourselves and change the way we look gives us another way to see ourselves not measuring up. Being able to imagine how our worlds would change if we looked a little different allows us to chase an ideal without any satisfaction.

What Makes a Body Image "Disturbed"

Professionals interested in body image problems often refer to struggles with body image as *body image disturbance*. Folks have talked about what this disturbance involves, however, in different ways.

Some have focused on how upsetting our body experiences can be. If, as you experienced your body in the last exercises, you felt sad or nervous or disgusted or ashamed or overwhelmed, psychologists might call this *body image distress*.

Others have focused on the inaccuracies of how we experience our bodies. If, in those last exercises, you saw your body differently than anyone else sees you, flaws seeming more obvious and terrible than anyone else would say, psychologists might call this *body image distortion*.

Some emphasize the distinction between what we consider perfect and what we see in the mirror. If, as you looked at your body, you found yourself comparing your appearance to some distant ideal, psychologists might call this *body image dissatisfaction.*

All of these seem to be at least a part of what many who struggle with body image experience. If you found your way this far into this book, it's likely that you've known the hurt that can come from not seeing what you want to see in the mirror. It's also likely that you've been told that what you see is not how others see you or that this shouldn't be such a big deal to you.

Unfortunately, our struggles with body image often don't stay put inside our heads in what we see, how we feel about what we see, or what we wish we saw. If you're reading these words right now, you've probably also felt your life bending in little ways around trying to keep that struggle with the way you think and feel and see your body under control.

Look back to the exercises you've done so far. If you noticed yourself skipping over parts of your body, imagining your body the way you wish it was, or skipping the exercise altogether, psychologists might call this *body image avoidance.* If you noticed yourself wanting to compare your actual reflection to what you imagined, psychologists might call this *body checking.* If you noticed that your body image brings up thoughts about your health, your relationships, your overall success, psychologists might call this *body image investment.* These all point to the ways that, without some action, our struggles with body image grow and grow until they are taking up more time and attention and energy than we'd ever dreamed.

Body Image Inflexibility

When taken together, these different terms suggest that body image disturbance involves:

- narrowed attention to certain aspects of appearance

- consistently painful thoughts and feelings about the body

- efforts to find relief from body-related thoughts and feelings

This is broadly referred to as *body image inflexibility*. Take a moment now and see if you don't recognize what body image inflexibility feels like from the inside out. You're moving along in your life and suddenly, something pulls your attention toward your body. Maybe it's something on the outside like a glimpse of your reflection or a comment on your outfit. It could be something on the inside like the feeling of your clothing pressing against you or the thought of finding an outfit for some event. Or maybe something happens that has nothing to do with your body but somehow sends your mind there. And hurt starts to come up—shame or disappointment or disgust or nervousness. And the more hurt that comes up, the more the rest of the world goes away. And you start to do things, little things, to get away from that hurt or to keep it from getting worse.

Over time, you've probably developed all kinds of ways of keeping this hurt at bay—strategies psychologists might call *body image avoidance*. You probably have some little things you do every day to manage how you feel about your appearance. You probably also have some more extreme things you do when you just can't shake the shame or disappointment. If you're willing, take a few moments now to consider where body image inflexibility shows up in your life and what your own struggle with body image looks like.

PRACTICE: When, Where, and What You Do About It

Take a deep breath and let your eyes come closed. Feel the gentle in and out of your breath for a few moments, just breathing.

Next let your mind roll over your day, from the moment your eyes come open and your awareness of the day floods in to the moment you drift away in sleep. See yourself moving about your world—the different places you go, the different people you meet.

And as you watch yourself in your life, see if you don't notice those tiny moments when your mind is swept away by your body, if even for an instant. And if you get to a moment when that shame or disgust or disappointment or fear around your body starts to rise up, hover there for just a moment. And as you hover, breathing in and out, make note that this is a hard space for you, a place you struggle.

And now, take just a moment to watch yourself in that hard place before moving on to the next thing. See if you can't recognize how you must be struggling inside. Notice the way your struggle shows up on the outside. The way your face or body changes. The way you hold yourself or move. The way you communicate with those around you. The places you let yourself go and the things you let yourself do. Spend just a moment noticing the shape your struggle takes.

Take a few moments to list some situations in which body image inflexibility shows up and what that struggle looks like for you. Try drawing a line down your page and writing on the left side, on every fourth or fifth line, a situation in which you get really inflexible with your body image. On the right side of each situation you list, write down what you tend to do in that situation. There are a couple of examples below. Ask yourself: When is body image inflexibility most likely to show up and take over in your life? What kinds of things do you do when it happens? What different ways have you found to keep your body image at bay? For example:

When I need to give a presentation: I notice that I spend extra time grooming, rush through, and forget to make eye contact.

When I'm invited out with friends for an evening: I don't go unless I have to, and I drink too much.

When I'm around my mother: I try to hide my flaws and eat too much, too quickly.

Try it yourself. We'll wait.

Now look over your list. Notice how many different things you do that are part of body image inflexibility for you—the things you wrote and all the things you didn't write. The things you are just now starting to notice you do. The things you are just now starting to realize are part of your struggle.

See if you can't let yourself wonder, really wonder, how many more you might come up with if you kept right on struggling with this. How many new ways would you find to run or hide or fight your own body image if you let this fill your life to your last day? For most people the answer is "thousands upon thousands upon thousands." Most of us could spend a lifetime saving ourselves from our own body image. And many of us do. Many of us have.

The Price We Pay to Struggle with Body Image

It's likely that this has something to do with the reason you picked up this book. Something about the way that this struggle was starting to fill your life was just not right for you. First, those things you do when body image inflexibility takes over have consequences in your life. Take a moment to look over each of them. Some of them are probably fine; they get you through a tough moment with your body with little impact on the rest of your life. But some of those things you wrote about (and maybe some things you couldn't bear to write) have real costs in your life. What kinds of costs do you see in the list you wrote above? What kinds of things have you sacrificed to this struggle?

If you're noticing that your struggle with body image is not just about your body, you're not alone. For many folks, body image inflexibility spreads out into other aspects of their lives. Your struggle with body image makes it more likely, for example, that you struggle with heart problems, breathing problems, or headaches

(Muennig et al. 2008). It also makes you more likely to use drugs or alcohol in ways that disrupt your life (Grant et al. 2005; Vickers et al. 2004). You are likely to find yourself struggling to keep your mood stable, with the threat of depression always lurking about (Armatas, Holt, and Rice 2003; Downs, DiNallo, and Kirner 2008; Forrest and Stuhldreher 2007; Stice et al. 2000). You might be steadily plagued by anxiety that nips at your ankles just enough to keep you running and tired of running (Leary and Kolwalski 1995; Phillips and Castle 2002). You're more likely to find yourself working too hard at your relationships, scrambling to make up for the ways in which you fall short, or defending your insecurities tirelessly (Cohen, Gottlieb, and Underwood 2000). Your struggle with body image even makes it more likely that you have chunks of time when you find yourself thinking a lot about death or suicide (Crow et al. 2008; Phillips et al. 2005).

Many of us have spent far too much of our time trying to fix this problem with body image—once and for all, or at least long enough for a small breath of relief. Many of us have felt the cost of that struggle in our physical health, our work, our relationships with others, and our relationships with ourselves.

Many of us would do almost anything to be released from this struggle. But who or what releases us? When is the battle over? How will we know when it's safe? And, moreover, is this even a struggle that can be won? Look back at the things you've done to change your body image. Have you not worked hard enough? Have you not wanted release bad enough? When is it time for you to start living your life the way you would choose?

If this were some other book, this would be the part when we unveiled the answer you've been looking for: The ultimate solution. The one thing you haven't tried. The finishing move in your life-long fight with body image—the one that puts the pain, and the disgust, and the nagging concerns, and the life-consuming efforts to bed. We'd point out how you've been thinking wrong or feeling wrong or acting wrong, and we'd give you ways to change that.

And this is not that book.

We are pretty sure we could give you tips on how to struggle better with your body image. Except here's the deal: you'd still be struggling! This book is about trying something different, something that's neither fixing your body nor fixing your body image. This book is about setting down your struggle with body image and living for something more than how you look or how you feel about how you look.

PRACTICE: The Next Moment

Take a moment to imagine that one night, as you slept, your struggle with body image were to suddenly just fall away. Let your eyes close and draw a slow, deep breath. Imagine you woke up and as you drew your eyes open and started moving around, you noticed that your struggle with body image had gone. You'd pause for a moment and wonder if it really could be true... and sure enough, you'd find that the struggle just wasn't there. Watch yourself in that moment of noticing that you are finally free. Now what would you do in the very next moment? How would you use that time? Where would you go? Who would you seek out? Take a moment to really see yourself moving about your world with freedom. Where would you bring yourself? What would you let yourself do? And breathe.

Take a moment to let yourself wonder—

How would you fill your day if you weren't bound by your body image?

Jot down a few things you would do if your struggle with body image were to suddenly go away. Then take a moment to read over the things you have written, one by one, slowly noticing what comes up as you read them. How does it feel to imagine yourself moving around your world with freedom? Take a moment and ask yourself what it would be like to start building that life right now, one little step at a time...

A Focus on Living

We're writing this book, right now, because we know what it's like: to wake up one morning and realize that whole chunks of your life are consumed by the struggle with your body. To look around and recognize that the things you're pouring your time and energy into are not the things that are most important, but the things that are most scary. Like you, we have come, over and over, to those moments of wondering how we came to be living like this—without a real sense of meaning or direction or richness. We have noticed ourselves still going, still living, day after day, but *merely* living.

And we think that folks deserve better.

We think that you deserve better.

And we think that we can do better.

This book is about choosing what better living looks like for you, noticing how your struggle with body image takes you away from that, and shifting your focus from struggling and merely living to living a life that matters to you. It's okay if you're not quite sure if that's possible for you, right for you, or even what you'd want. We do hope, however, that you might let yourself wonder what that might mean for you, and that you'll join us as we tell you a little bit more about what we are offering.

2 Letting Go of the Struggle

As we said before, the work we are offering in this book is based on an approach to psychotherapy called *acceptance and commitment therapy*, or ACT. ACT is a little different from most other therapies because it wasn't developed to help folks with a certain disorder. Rather, the research and theory behind ACT suggest that all people struggle in one way or another at different times in their lives, and that our natural human response to difficulties causes us to struggle way longer and way harder than we need to.

ACT has been shown to be helpful to people with all sorts of struggles (Hayes et al. 2006). It has been successfully applied to helping people diagnosed with the kinds of struggles we call psychological disorders—struggles like depression (Zettle and Hayes 1986; Zettle and Rains 1989), anxiety (Eifert et al. 2009), and even psychosis (Gaudiano and Herbert 2006; Bach and Hayes 2002). And ACT isn't just about psychological disorders. The same model has also been helpful to folks with health problems like chronic pain (McCracken, Vowles, and Eccleston 2004), diabetes (Gregg et al. 2007), and epilepsy (Lundgren et al. 2006). And it's not just useful for folks with psychological or medical problems. ACT can also stand for *acceptance and commitment training* when it's helping folks who wouldn't necessarily be diagnosed with anything. ACT has been shown to help people work with fewer workplace errors (Moran 2011), achieve better in school (Brown et al. 2011), build better relationships (Peterson et al. 2009), and improve at public speaking (England et al. 2012).

There's really not a big difference, from an ACT perspective, between how different kinds of struggles come to take over our lives. There's also not a big difference, from an ACT perspective, on how it is we take our lives back.

Psychological Flexibility as Psychological Well-Being

One thing that makes ACT different from other approaches to therapy is the way we think of psychological well-being. Many approach psychological health the way we would physical health. How do we know if our bodies are healthy? We look for problems, and if we don't find any problems, then that's physical health. So, physical health is often defined as the absence of physical problems.

For a long time, psychological health was looked at pretty much the same way. It was defined by the absence of psychological problems, and problems were experiences like frustration, disappointment, anxiety, and self-doubt. Difficult thoughts and feelings were approached as indications that something was wrong. And if, when we looked around, nothing much seemed too wrong out in the world, then the problem was with us.

Psychological Flexibility

In ACT, psychological health is not defined by the absence of difficult thoughts or feelings. It's defined by the way we respond to difficult thoughts and feelings. Research findings are converging from a variety of sources to suggest that psychological health is about flexibility (Hayes, Strosahl, and Wilson 1999; Kashdan and Rottenberg 2010): Flexibility in the way we experience the world, inside and out. Flexibility in the way we take perspective. Flexibility in the way we use what is available to us to achieve what we want. Flexibility in the way we move about our ever-changing world.

In ACT, we emphasize *psychological flexibility* as a fundamental quality of psychological health. The person experiencing depression doesn't have trouble living because he feels sad or empty. He has trouble living because when he feels sad or empty, he turns away from his world. The person with anxiety doesn't have trouble living because she feels fearful or tense. She has trouble living because when she feels fearful or tense, she can only bear to go certain places. And the person with body image difficulties doesn't find her world slipping away because she hates the way she looks. She finds her world slipping away because she is constantly trying to manage the way she feels about the way she looks.

What if you can learn to be aware of and open to your experience, as lovely or as terrible as it may be, and continue moving toward things that matter to you? What if, instead of struggling with body image, you can learn to be aware of and open to your body experiences, as pleasant or painful as they may be, and continue moving toward the life you want to have?

Valued Living

The primary purpose in ACT is exactly this: living a life that moves you closer and closer to being the person that you want to be. We think that the specific ways that you struggle are less important than the specific ways that you would choose to be living if this struggle weren't taking over.

Look back at your exercise at the very end of the last chapter. If your struggle with body image were to suddenly fall away one day, where would you spend your time? Are there people that you would want to be sure to see—to share that freedom with? Is there something you'd want to do with your body—a dance, a run, an embrace? Would you take that time to soak up nature, to focus on your education, or to really pour yourself into your job in a way you haven't before? Is there something you've been longing to express that you might have the courage to say, or write, or draw, or build? Would you take that time to grow a little in your spirituality, your wisdom, your health?

If suddenly all that time and energy you spend on your body image were available to spend on other things, how would you choose to spend it? Spend a few moments in that question, noticing what comes up. And then, if you're willing, bring that sense of the life you'd value to bear in the next exercise.

PRACTICE: The Life You'd Value

Whenever you're ready, take a few moments and consider important areas in your life such as family, career, and the arts. Then look at them one at a time, moving gently from one to the next. Stop at each domain briefly and let yourself wonder what really living that value all the way would mean for you. What would you choose to change about the way you approach that part of your life?

If you started making changes in that area, changes that really mattered, what would folks see? Notice what your valued actions would look like from the outside.

If you started making changes in that area, what would you feel? Notice how your valued actions would feel from the inside.

Now take a moment to jot down at least one extraordinary thing you could make happen in each domain of life you listed.

When you've finished, give yourself a couple of breaths and notice which domains of life are most important to you, what hopes you have for yourself in these areas, what fears or concerns you carry with you there, and how that's reflected in or conflicts with the way you are currently living your life.

Now, if you're willing, set a timer for ten minutes and write about one or two domains of life that you value. As you write, imagine that your thoughts could pour directly from your mind onto the page. When you find yourself struggling with what to say next or how exactly to say what you mean, see if you can't set that struggle aside and return to the task at hand—expressing some sense of what it is that you care about.

Read over the things that you've written. And before we move on to the next thing, take a moment now to notice what other thoughts and feelings come up when you think about the things that matter to you. Take a slow breath and see what might show up right inside of that sense of meaning. Is there a kernel of longing in there? Of regret? Of disappointment or frustration?

For most of us, working on things that matter little to us is way easier than working on things that matter deeply. Once we reach out for something we really want, we become aware of the risk of messing up, the risk of losing it forever. The things we are asking of you in this book are difficult, but they are not difficult for nothing.

It's Your Life, Through Your Eyes

If this piece of work we've laid out in this book were to serve you exactly as we hope, it would help you to make changes in the way you carry your body image. Not just any changes—changes that would really matter to you. Changes that would help you to move steadily forward into the life that you care about. Notice that this is going to mean something a little different for you than for every other person who picks up this book. The life that would be most meaningful to you won't be built of the same pieces as the life that would be most meaningful for your dad or your best friend or your coworker.

Also notice that this work is not about us telling you what you're doing wrong or how you should be living. Built right inside of psychological flexibility is the idea that change is hard and only worth it if it *matters* for something. This work is not about building the life we would pick for you. Not the life your mother or partner or teacher or coach or sibling or grandfather would want for you. It's about the life you would choose, if you could turn and behold all of the many possibilities laid out before you and simply pick the life you wanted.

This means that, if this work is going to really serve you, it's not going to be about rejecting things you've known and just trusting what we say is true. Let's say that again: it's *not* about rejecting your experience and just trusting us. In fact, we're thinking sort of the opposite. We think, if this work is going to serve you, it's going to be about receiving the things we have to offer openly, then checking out your own experience to see how these things work for you. We can only guess at the pain you've carried and the direction you might choose to head. But those are the details that are going to help you choose what this shift is actually going to look like for you.

Another way of saying this is that we are going to trust that you have everything you need to build the life that you want for yourself, to be the person you want to be. We think what we're doing is offering you a little space and time to put those resources to work. You've probably already noticed that we are going to ask you to do difficult things in this book—things that might be completely contrary to how you've worked with body image in the past. Know that when we ask these things of you, it's always because we have some sense that stepping into that difficulty, and doing it in a new way, could move you toward something that matters to you. It's always in your hands to wonder what that something might be and how it is or is not worth that step forward. And... you can always step back.

Body Image Flexibility and Four Opportunities for Change

This book is about helping you to practice noticing and experiencing your body image while choosing other things, more important things, to focus your life around. We call this psychological flexibility with your body image, or *body image flexibility*. Notice that this is the other side of the body image inflexibility we talked about in the last chapter. Also notice, though, that body image flexibility is not defined by things you don't experience or do. It's defined in terms of a set of skills.

As you might imagine, the mere act of reading our words on these pages, or even spending a few minutes here and there practicing, is not likely to affect your life unless you extend your practice out into your life. This is not, however, always as easy as it sounds. In part, it's because most of us have never thought much about body image flexibility as an option. It's sort of like we've all been playing soccer and wondering why things aren't going right on the basketball court. Practicing basketball is not going to help unless we shift what we are doing on the court from soccer to basketball.

So, we think that, like any skill, body image flexibility is something to be practiced. It's not a thing you do once and for all that changes your relationship with your body image forever. It's something you do over and over, getting better and better at it, so that you can have it as an option when there are important things at stake.

Look back at the situations you wrote about in the last chapter—times when hurt over your body comes up most for you. Notice what you tend to do in those hard spots. What if you started doing something a little different in those moments, such as hesitating just long enough to notice, or stepping into things you usually fight or run or hide from? If you string enough of those tiny chosen steps together, what you have is a life of choice, a life you've built.

We think of this practice of body image flexibility in terms of all the things people do that threaten that valued life. The next section of this book will review four ways that your body image can start to get in the way of your life. We'll show you how these moments of body image inflexibility are four opportunities for change. You'll be invited to look at how, where, when, and why inflexibility comes up in your life and to practice doing something different.

When things get hard, people tend to lose sight of the things that matter. That's why your suggested practice will involve choosing a direction for your life. During tough times, people also tend to notice less and less of what's going on around them and within them. So we'll show you how to practice just noticing your experience. You may also tend to let your thoughts and feelings about yourself and the world stand in for the actual world. So your practice will involve experiencing the world beyond your thoughts about the world. Sometimes you will find yourself working pretty hard to protect yourself from certain parts of your experience that hurt instead of going for the things you really want. So your practice will involve opening up to that hurt when it means you get closer to those things that matter to you. Finally, when you get knocked down, it's very hard to hop up and take that next step. So your practice will involve taking tiny steps into the life you want, noticing when you start running away, and turning back.

You've actually already started practicing body image flexibility. In the very last practice, you took some time choosing a life you'd value, a life that is more important to you than your thoughts and feelings about your body. This is the purpose of acceptance and commitment therapy and other approaches that aim for body image flexibility. And that life you dared to hope for, the life you wrote about—that will be our purpose throughout this book.

In the next four chapters, we'll invite you to practice four opportunities to change your way of interacting with your body (and the rest of the world):

- *being present,* or noticing your ongoing experiences of your body and the world as they occur in and around you

- *seeing beyond your thoughts,* or noticing your thoughts about your body without letting them dominate your experience

- *accepting experience,* or opening up to those dominating thoughts and the feelings that come with them

- *getting to know you,* or contacting the you that is more than the way you see, feel, and think about your body

With each opportunity for change that we introduce, we'll invite you to take some time to practice. First, you'll practice safely with our book, trying on new things and watching how they work. Then, you'll bring this work out into your life. In each chapter, you'll make commitments to set the book down and go about living. And if your commitments are bold, if they're true to what you want, you'll be creating the life you care about, the person that you want to be, taking one step at a time, and turning back when you find that you've turned away from your commitments.

If all this isn't making a whole lot of sense to you right now... well, good. That means you're probably paying attention. This approach is different from the way most of us believe thinking, and feeling, and living are supposed to work. So it's not always going to feel totally straightforward. In fact, sometimes it might feel downright backward. We think, though, that if the way you've always thought about this stuff was going to help you through it, you wouldn't be reading this book.

Okay, you might be thinking, *So this work is going to be hard, and it's not always going to make sense... now why exactly should I keep reading?* Well, the answer to that question depends on you. Take a moment and look back at your last practice exercise. Read what you wrote carefully, noticing what thoughts and feelings come up for you as you do. Think back to the other exercises you've done so far.

Notice the difference in your experience between when you are focusing on your body versus when you are calling up your values. Amongst all the things that matter to you, is there one thing that you value that would be worth encountering the most difficult of your thoughts and feelings? If you're willing, we invite you to pick one value that you'd be willing to work toward with this book and write it down: "I value…"

Let yourself notice the pull to reach out for that value, to make changes to bring you toward it. And without turning away from that pull, notice if a part of you doesn't want to push that value away, to not think about it too much. And now, think about your struggle with body image. Are there ways that your struggle with body image interferes with this value? Below where you wrote down what you value, write a few words about how your struggle with body image moves you away from your value.

Now let yourself consider how you might want to commit to this piece of work in service of that value. Maybe you'd like to work through one chapter a week, or one every two weeks. Maybe you'd be willing to read and practice for twenty minutes a day. Maybe you'd like to do ten minutes during the week, thirty minutes on Saturdays, and nothing on Sundays. Maybe you've only got two pages a week in you. Take a moment to let all the possibilities bubble up before you. Think about what it is you might be willing to commit to if it brought you closer toward that value. It's totally up to you. This is not the kind of thing somebody can do for you. It's also not the kind of question to which there is a right answer. You get to pick.

Now, before you write anything more down, notice what shows up as you start thinking about a commitment. Maybe there's some excitement. Maybe you feel yourself on the edge of a piece of work that could really matter for your life. Maybe you feel a little nervous. Maybe you notice yourself trying to sort out what the perfect commitment would be. Maybe you feel annoyed at even being asked to commit. Maybe you notice the urge to flip past this page and get to the new chapter more quickly.

For most of us, the issue of commitment is tangled up with all kinds of other difficult stuff. And it's no wonder. In most situations in your life, once you make a commitment or a promise, it's supposed to somehow direct your behavior, such that you never turn away from it. And that's not even the scariest thing about commitment. Worse still is that if you do turn away, if you find yourself not fulfilling that commitment, if you get distracted or lose your way, that means that somehow you never committed in the first place. In most situations, somehow your action today can actually go back in time and break your commitment. No wonder people have commitment issues!

In ACT, we look at commitment a little differently. Our question is never whether or not we will ever turn away. The thing we are most interested in is the turning back. When we do turn away, how quickly do we turn back? What if the job of being committed simply means that you will notice when you are doing things that interfere with your values, and shift to doing something that moves you toward them? What if the guy who screws up a hundred times but always comes back to his commitment is no less committed than the guy who only screws up and comes back once?

With this in mind, choose a commitment that defines what your work with this book might look like and write it down: "I commit to…"

Now breathe. Literally. Give yourself a couple of deep breaths. This work is not easy, and if you are still reading, you deserve some acknowledgment. We've asked about the most difficult struggles in your life and your most precious values. Calling that up and writing it down is difficult, even if you know no one will be reading it. Yet here we are.

And if you've sort of skipped through, reading without doing any of the practices, that's okay, too. Go ahead and read the whole thing that way if you like. And then, if there's any little part of you that thinks there could be something to this, get yourself a notebook and some earbuds or headphones, turn back to the beginning, and start working through the practices.

In the next section, we'll invite you to practice each of the four opportunities for change that are part of body image flexibility one at a time. We hope you'll join us. We are truly honored to be able to be a part of this work for you.

Part 2

FOUR OPPORTUNITIES FOR CHANGE

3 Right Here, Right Now: Being Present

Stefanie feels her chest start to tighten as she steps into the house and the beautiful, smiling woman takes her coat. She smiles back widely, painfully aware that her teeth are not nearly so white as this woman's whose name she can't seem to recall. Stefanie is reminding herself to breathe and noticing how tight her dress feels around her chest when she realizes the woman has just asked her something. "Oh yes," she says, hoping she caught the gist of the question, "It's been just great." She turns away too quickly to see the woman's reaction. Stefanie walks into the crowd, feeling increasingly unstable in her new high heels. Her hand goes instinctively to her face and she brushes her hands over her skin to check for blemishes— forehead, right cheek, left cheek, chin. And suddenly Stefanie is fourteen, wobbling around her first formal in a dress she doesn't quite fill out, feeling like a little girl playing dress-up. *Just an ugly duckling,* she finds herself

thinking over and over, *and one day it'll all be different.*
The hand on her arm brings her back to the lights and
sounds of the party. Stefanie wonders if her arm feels
clammy, brings her hand to her head, and tries to focus
on the bearded man who's asking if she'd like a drink.

Well, here we are. Here in this single moment among an infinite
number of moments that could be, moments that have been,
moments that will be. Right now. In the present.

Or are we? For most of us, a little part of us is in the here, a
little slice of us is hovering in the now, but much of our attention is
elsewhere. As you read the words on this page, some of your attention is set aside for turning the squiggles into words and a bit of
your attention is devoted to making sense of those words. Some of
your attention is monitoring your body, letting you know when you
need to shift positions, or pull on a sweater, or get some water.
Some of your attention is holding the world around you, noting
when the air conditioner kicks on or the phone rings or someone
walks into the room.

And not only that: a whole other chunk of your attention is on
the stuff unfolding in your own mind. Some attention is dedicated
to evaluating and comparing what you are reading with other stuff.
You might think, *I don't quite get what this means. Is this like that
other book I read on body image? I just don't know if this is going to be
helpful. What if I spent all this time and nothing was different? Wait,
this sounds right. Oh, I get this. Yeah, it's totally like that. Wow, I never
thought of it that way. Do I do this? Is this like what happened last
week?*

Or sometimes what's unfolding in your mind has nothing to do
with what you are reading. You might be reading everything, word
by word, while much of your attention is going over a conversation
from yesterday, planning what you need to pack for a weekend trip,
or making a list of the clothes that need to go to the cleaners
tomorrow.

And that's not all. Some of your attention is set aside for watching your feelings unfold. A little excitement flowing into worry flowing into disappointment flowing into hope flowing back into excitement flowing into anxiety and then into frustration... In fact, with each breath, any number of thoughts and feelings pass through us more quickly than we can even track.

You can imagine that all of your attention is chopped up into rooms like a busy corporate headquarters and that you sit somewhere where you can see into every room. Imagine a security headquarters with great big screens lining one wall, each one a monitor catching everything going on in a room. And sitting there, in your office, you can peek from this monitor to that, watching and hearing whatever is going on in any one moment.

So it is with all of the experiences in our attention. At any one moment your attention is filled with everything you're hearing and seeing and smelling and feeling and thinking. And at any one moment, you can shift your awareness among any of those aspects of your experience. See if you don't notice a gentle shift of your attention as you read the words on this page. Sense the sounds rising and falling around you, the scents on the air, the movement and light in the room.

Notice that the sounds in the room or tastes in your mouth might be available in some part of your attention, but that doesn't mean that your awareness is there. You can tune in, or out, to anything you're thinking or feeling or perceiving. Let's try an example. Take a moment right now to notice all of the sensations in your hand. See if you can't get every little detail. The temperature on your hand. Anything pressing against it. The weight of your hand itself. Any pain that is there. Stop reading for a moment. Stop, close your eyes, and just shift all of your awareness to the sensations in one of your hands for five slow breaths.

What just happened? Before you were instructed to pay attention to the sensations in your hands, were they there? Certainly the nerves in your hand were sensing stuff before you shifted your awareness there. Yet, unless you were experiencing some discomfort in your hand, you probably weren't very aware of it. You weren't tuned in to that monitor. Just like you may not really be aware of the air conditioner sound until it suddenly turns off or that you are making noises with your pen until someone asks you to stop.

For most of us, our awareness sort of bounces from this to that without much control on our part. Consider the example of driving. If the weather is fine and your car's running well and it's a route you usually take, you're not likely to spend a whole lot of time watching the signs you pass or the trees that line the street or even the cars around you and the traffic signals. These things have some of your attention, or else you would have far more accidents than you do, but your awareness can float around to other things. So the monitor that shows signs and trees and cars and signals is there, but you're not leaned in, tracking every change.

Instead you're with another monitor, perhaps counting days until vacation. Or one where you're comparing your belly to that of a person you see crossing the street. You might glance over at the monitor to your left and let yourself really be absorbed by going over and over an annoying conversation you had with your mother yesterday. Then you might lean back and be grabbed suddenly by a text message you weren't expecting. Then when that settles down, you do a quick scan to see what's happening on each monitor, one by one, before settling in on what you might wear to the party next weekend and when you might find time to get some shopping done.

How It Goes: Scattered or Stuck

That's how the human mind works: your awareness is constantly shifting direction and focus among all the pieces of your experience—including hearing, smelling, feeling, remembering—in any one moment. For most folks, though, this shifting is not always the gentle, easy process we describe above. For most of us, our awareness tends to shift in one of two ways: scattered or stuck.

When Awareness Is Scattered

Sometimes, awareness leaps quickly from this to that. The tiniest shift in the environment pulls all your awareness in that direction. The air conditioner kicks on and all your awareness is with the rumbling above you. Until the next moment, when the light changes slightly in the room and all your awareness is out the window with the shifting trees. Until the next moment, when your phone beeps that you have a text. Until the next moment, when you wonder whether or not you should text back. Until the next moment, when you notice the time on the phone and bring your awareness back to your work. Until the next moment, when you imagine what would become of you if you failed at this work. Until the next moment, when the song you weren't really listening to ends and you can suddenly hear the clock's tick.

Most folks have experienced scattered awareness at some point. It might come with anxiety or with excitement. You're getting ready for something that's going to happen, but you can't keep your awareness in one place long enough to get anything done. It might come with intense emotions. You might find it hard to keep your awareness steady long enough to complete a logical thought. Scattered awareness sometimes comes with situations that are loud or bright or busy. The things going on around you might be so stimulating that your awareness shifts rapidly from that sound to this light to that sensation, with your thoughts and feelings rushing to catch up. For some of us, it doesn't seem to matter much what's going on around us or inside of us. Some of us struggle with scattered awareness most of the time. You may look around sometimes and notice that most people seem more focused than you ever feel.

For some, the quickly shifting attention feels like distractibility. You might feel "all over the place." You might say you're having a hard time focusing or concentrating. You might struggle to read for a long time and understand what you're reading. You might lose interest in conversations or activities right when others seem to be getting into it. You might have a hard time getting started on projects because you are so easily derailed into taking care of other things.

For others, this same rapid shifting of awareness feels workable or even necessary. You might notice that you feel more aware of what's going on around you or inside you than other people. You might be able to close your eyes at any moment and describe the objects and people around you. You might notice that you feel more aware of what's going on inside you than other people. You might, at any point, be able to describe exactly how your heart is beating or your breath is coming or your digestion is going at any one moment. Keeping track of certain parts of your experience might feel important because things can go wrong so easily. You might find yourself constantly scanning for things that are dangerous or threatening, and even being surprised or frustrated that others don't.

Is some of this sounding familiar? Take a moment and call to mind times or situations when your attention was scattered, and jot them down.

When Awareness Is Stuck

Sometimes, it's not that awareness is leaping quickly from this to that, it's that awareness can't seem to peel away from one aspect of experience. Something creeps into your attention and once it's there, you can't even turn away from it slightly for more than a moment or two. It might be that you notice the clock ticking and suddenly it seems like the loudest thing in the room. You might read about a condition that comes with trouble breathing and suddenly find yourself obsessing over whether or not you're breathing funny. More often than not, when awareness is stuck, it's stuck on stuff going on within us rather than around us.

Sometimes it starts as an unknown—a little something you're wondering about. *I wonder what everyone else will be wearing. I wonder who else will be there. I wonder how she liked my paper. I wonder if they like me. I wonder what things will be like when I graduate.* Then your wondering about unknowns slips into what-if's nagging at you. *What if I show up and all the other people are dressed in suits? What if no one I know is there? What if she hated my paper? What if they hate me? What if I never find my way?* And then nagging what-if's slip into worries (*How will it go?*) or ruminations (*What have I done?*) that seem to go on and on without really getting anywhere.

Once we start worrying about the future or ruminating over the past, our awareness can easily get stuck on that concern, with barely any shifting, and every other shift leading back to that concern. You might talk about being "preoccupied" or "zoned out." It's like you're not even in your world with the things you see and hear and smell and feel and taste. And the only thoughts that you hang on to are part of this worry loop. You're thinking about a conversation that went badly: imagining different ways it could have gone, wishing you'd done something different. Then a phone call breaks the spell, but even as the other person talks on the phone, you're back to rehearsing the ways you could have fixed it in your head. Then you stub your toe and you're suddenly back in the world, but as you hop around on one foot, you start to think about how you muck everything up, just like that conversation—you can't even walk without running into something. The sun breaks through the clouds into a particularly beautiful day, and then you're back with the conversation that went wrong. The song on the radio changes, then you're back with the conversation that went wrong. You calculate a bill, and then you're back. You say hi to someone, and then you're back. You spend forty minutes cleaning, and for the entire forty minutes you're playing out different things that could have happened and all the ways you'd fix it if you had a chance.

Take a moment and call to mind times or situations when your awareness was stuck, and jot them down.

Your Awareness

Now take a look at the notes you've made and think a little more about your own experience with your awareness. How does your awareness usually go? Are you someone who really struggles with being scattered? Are you someone whose awareness always seems to be stuck on something? Can you think of examples of both?

If you're finding it difficult to think about this stuff, you're not alone. If you're like most people, you've never really thought much about your awareness at all. You may have noticed that you tend to worry more or seem more scattered than others. You might feel on some days that you're really not all there. But noticing your own awareness in a moment-by-moment way—where it lies and how it shifts—is something that most of us never learn to do. For many of us, however, this can be the first step in directing our awareness in ways that work for us.

PRACTICE: Noticing Awareness

In this next practice, if you're willing, you'll take a few moments to try exactly this—just being aware of your awareness. If you're using the audio files that you can download to use with this book, you can go ahead and put on track 4 to guide you. (See the back of the book for download information, and go to www.newharbinger .com/21044 to get started.) This track will provide some brief instructions, and then will be mostly silent, with a bell sound every so often.

If you're not using the recordings, grab a timer, even on your watch or phone, and set it for thirty seconds. When the alarm sounds, first notice where your awareness lies... With something you hear? Something you see? Something you feel? Something you're thinking? Then notice what else is there, in your attention, that you could be aware of. If you were mostly aware of your leg itching, notice the feelings in your other leg, the sounds in the room, the words running through your mind. Then set the alarm for another thirty seconds. Do this six times for a total of three minutes. You don't need to close your eyes or breathe any certain way. During this practice, these three minutes, your job is simply to notice where your awareness lies at any one moment.

So what did you notice? Is your awareness scattered today? Did you bounce from one thing to the next? Is your awareness stuck today? Did you keep coming back to some concern you've got hanging around? What kinds of things seemed most compelling of your awareness? What was it like to try to notice all the other parts of your experience you weren't aware of? Does any of this remind you of how your awareness typically goes in your life?

Take a moment and jot down a few of your observations about what you noticed between tones, what you noticed when the tones sounded, and what, if anything, this practice reminded you of.

Awareness and Struggles with Body Image

Okay, you might be thinking, *so my awareness gets stuck sometimes and scattered others... What does that have to do with my body?* For many of us, our struggles with body image are apparent in how our awareness works. It's not that folks who struggle with body image get any more scattered or stuck than people who don't. It's that *when* you get stuck or scattered, it often has something to do with your body. And if it doesn't start that way, it often ends up there.

You may find that your awareness gets generally scattered or stuck when you're feeling particularly bad about your body. You feel disappointed with what you see in the mirror. You feel your clothes not fitting right on your body. You notice someone else with a trait you'd love to have. You're wearing an outfit you're not comfortable in. And while you're carrying all that discomfort, it's difficult to move your awareness about your world in the way you need to. You are either unable to tear your awareness away from the way your body feels or the way you imagine it looks, or you can't seem to settle your awareness on anything at all.

For some of us, our scattered awareness involves keeping tabs on different aspects of body awareness. We may have different aspects of how our bodies look and feel that we are constantly checking in on, one at a time. *Is my back straight? Is my belly tight? Is my makeup fresh? Are my clothes hanging right? Is my hat straight? Is my hair shiny? Is my skin smooth?* And it may seem that you are in a constant loop. Like Stefanie at the party, you're halfway in your world and halfway working through your worries and checks. You wonder, *Can they see what I'm hiding?*

For some of us, staying scattered keeps our awareness from settling on our bodies much at all. It may be that until you opened up this book, that was one slice of your experience, one monitor in the control room that rarely caught your awareness. It may be that until pretty recently you experienced your world on a day-to-day basis as if you didn't really have a body at all. And because awareness of our bodies—what's going on inside, what's touching us and how, where our parts are in space—is all pretty important stuff, staying away from letting it settle there means keeping a pretty frantic pace. It may be that if our awareness landed there, it'd be pretty tough to pull away.

Most folks who struggle with body image find it difficult to be aware of their bodies at all without getting stuck. Give yourself a slow, deep breath and ask yourself the following questions: When you look at a picture of yourself, where do your eyes settle first? When you are trying on a new outfit, what makes or breaks your decision to buy? When you catch your reflection, what do you see before anything else? If you close your eyes right now and imagine standing naked in front of a mirror, what part of the image hangs on the longest? In other words, what part of your body takes over what you see when you see you? For most of us, it's never the part of our bodies we don't care much about or the part of our appearance we're most proud of. It's the part we wish were different, the part we'd work to change, that our awareness tends to get stuck on.

And all this getting stuck and scattered means that, for those of us who struggle with body image, our overall experience of our bodies is limited. For some of us, the thing we struggle with the most is something we carry with us all the time and know very little about. You may have had the experience before of someone describing you as if they see something totally different from what you see. You feel terrible about how you look and someone says you're looking great. You might even point out exactly what you're dissatisfied with and it's like they just can't see it. For some time, psychologists believed that folks who struggle with body image somehow saw exaggerated versions of the parts of their bodies they didn't like. Then research showed that it's not that they see anything different from what others see, it's that that is *all* they see. Your friend who tells you that you look beautiful tonight might be compelled by how your outfit brings out your eye color, while all you see is that part of your body you hate.

Take a moment and jot down the part (or parts) of your body that your awareness gets stuck on.

Costs of the Struggle with Body Awareness

Unfortunately, struggles with body awareness don't just limit the body experience. They limit all experience. The problem with struggling with body awareness is that the things that you care about, your chosen values, are more important than your body. And when your awareness is scattered or stuck, you miss stuff. Call to mind the last time you were feeling really terrible about your body. See if you can recall what it was like to try to be in your skin that day. Did you stay in touch with the world around you? Were you able to connect with the people in your life? Were you able to make moment-to-moment choices toward the life you want? Did you take action, following through with the choices you made? And as you try to remember now, notice this: How much of your experience never made it into your memory to begin with?

What if it's the case that, in any moment, your whole world is filled with opportunities? And not just any opportunities—opportunities to really step into your life, to take hold of the things that matter to you. Opportunities to begin building the life you want, a life where you can begin to grow into the person you want to be. And what if, in the same way that you might miss instructions for what to do next or signs for your next interstate exit when you are scattered or stuck, it's also true that opportunities can pass without you ever really being aware of them?

What opportunities might Stefanie have missed in just those few minutes at the party? What opportunities might you have missed?

PRACTICE: What Have You Missed?

Call to mind once more what it's like when you feel really awful about your body. This is going to be hard, because you can't really let yourself make contact with what it's like to feel awful without feeling awful all over again. We're asking you to do it anyway, though, just in case there's something meaningful in doing it a little differently. And if there's not, you can always shove it back out of your mind. Take a moment and jot down things you may miss because your awareness is scattered or stuck.

Now take a look over the list you've created, letting yourself imagine, one by one, how it would feel if these things gradually dropped out of your life instead of just your awareness. Next, mark each missed event you wrote down as follows:

> *1. Draw one line through the things you're okay with missing, the things that don't hold much value for you.*

2. *Underline the things you'd rather not miss, the things you want in your life.*

3. *Circle the things you really value, the things you'd work to keep in your life.*

Next we are going to describe an alternative to being scattered or stuck, but before we do, we want to acknowledge that change is hard. In fact, changing our behavior usually isn't worth doing if it isn't *for* something. So before we step into this next part, it's worth considering what you'd be doing this *for*. Take a look at the things you underlined and the things you circled, and ask yourself if those things are worth trying something different. If there's a chance they are, we invite you to consider what we call *being present*.

An Alternative: Being Present

Most of us, on most days and for most of the day, spend the moments that compose our lives only partway present. Our awareness shifts from this to that, yanked here and then bouncing there, then getting stuck tight on that other thing, then snapping back to this here. And while this is what we usually do, it is not what we *have* to do.

What if there is a completely different way we can connect with the world around us and inside us? What if we can, at any moment, pause and begin noticing our experiences unfolding in the moment? Noticing the sounds around us, the scents on the air, the temperature in the room, the sensations that comprise our breathing. What if one reason that your struggle with your body gets away from you is that you're not all the way there to begin with?

There has long been a place in many spiritual and cultural traditions for practicing being present. In the psychological flexibility model, this means maintaining awareness that is flexible in both direction and focus. From this perspective, being present means intentionally noticing the sensations around and inside you, along with the thoughts and feelings that come up with every shift in sensation. It means being able to hold your awareness to one aspect of experience, guiding it back when it slips away, and being able to shift your awareness gently among your experiences with intention. It means being able to broaden your awareness to allow more in or narrow your focus to notice every detail of one aspect of your experience.

In some ways, being present means doing all the shifting and narrowing and broadening your awareness does anyway, but on purpose. Being present means taking hold of your awareness and moving it with intention instead of the world shoving and yanking and bouncing it from this to that. And this return to the present is something you can do in any moment, in any situation. And it's something you will do over and over and over, every time you find yourself drifting away, if being present is something you are willing to try.

Being Present to the Body: Building Body Awareness

The body is, like any other aspect of your world, a constantly changing experience. Your skin provides a constant flow of information about the contact between your body and the world—the heat, the cold, where there is light touch, where there is deep pressure, where there is pain. Your muscles and joints are constantly telling you where all your body parts are and how they are moving. Special organs in your ears keep track of how your head is positioned in relation to the world beneath you. In every moment of your life, you are experiencing your world from inside your own unique body that only you can ever know.

And not only can you feel the world through it, you can look upon your body as the world does. Your body is always there, on the edges of what you see—hands moving as you talk, chest rising and falling with each breath, feet shooting out from under you as you walk. And, when so compelled, you can turn and face yourself in a reflection, seeing the eyes you peer through, the mouth you use to breathe and sing and eat. You can trace your shape with your eyes in the mirror. You can watch your shape change as you move. In every moment of your life, you can look down or look into a mirror and see the body you carry with you.

Applied to body image struggles, being present means practicing awareness of your unfolding experience of your body. What if the first step to letting go of that struggle is to make contact with what it is you are actually struggling with? You already did a little bit of noticing your body experience in the first chapter. The challenge now is to build body awareness as a skill.

Returning to the Body

Being present is not a one-time thing you decide to be and so you are. It's also not a matter of working hard enough on it until you cross some threshold and are forever changed. Being present would more accurately be named *returning to the present*, because it involves noticing when you are scattered or when you are stuck, and beginning to direct your awareness with intention. Your body is a unique aspect of your moment-to-moment experience because it is something that is always there for you to return to. This ongoing sensory experience that is your body holds an invitation to return, over and over, to the now. And returning your awareness to your body, in the now, can mean bringing it back to the life you care about.

This next practice will involve exactly this—bringing your awareness gently to your body experience, and returning when you find your awareness getting scattered or stuck. The practice will happen in two parts, the first focusing on body image from the inside out, and the second including body image from the outside in. If you're following along on the audio files that came with this book, please play track 5 at this time.

PRACTICE: Returning to the Body, Part I

Take a moment to draw a slow, deep breath. Let your eyes fall closed. And as you breathe, let your attention come to rest on the sensation of breathing. Notice how it feels to draw the air into your body. Notice the temperature of the air hitting your nose or lips on the way in and notice it again as you push the air out. Notice the way the muscles expand to pull the air in and squeeze together to push the air out. And breathe.

And now gently guide your attention to the sounds of your breath. Notice the sounds of the air as it rushes past your lips or nose. Notice the subtle shifts in volume, the texture of the sound. Take a moment to listen for any other tiny sounds of your breathing—such as your clothes shifting slightly as your belly expands. And breathe.

And when you have a sense of what it feels like and sounds like to breathe, gently expand your attention out to take in your bodily experience more broadly. See if you can't wrap your awareness around the whole of your physical presence as it is right now. And breathe.

Take a moment here to notice the differences in temperature in your body. Let your attention come to rest on the parts of your body that feel cold. Notice each of those cold spots, one by one, letting your attention come to rest on the coldest. And breathe.

Now let your attention come to rest on the parts of your body that feel warm. If more than one area feels warm, notice each one in turn, letting your attention come to rest on the warmest. And breathe.

Take a moment now to notice any pressure on your skin. Notice areas of light pressure, maybe where your clothes barely brush on your skin. Notice areas of more firm pressure, where your bottom touches the chair or where elastic in your clothing binds your skin. See if you can't notice the lightest touch you feel on your skin right now. And see if you can't notice the firmest pressure on your skin right now. And breathe.

And now let your attention shift into your muscles. Notice any tension in your muscles, any places your muscles feel tight and engaged. Let your attention come to rest on each of these areas of tension one by one. And breathe.

Now, notice any areas of relaxation, any places where your muscles feel heavy and tingling. Let your attention come to rest on each of these areas of relaxation one by one. And breathe.

Take a moment now to notice any body or head pain you are carrying with you today. Let your attention come to rest there, on that pain. Notice if there is a shape or a rhythm to that pain. Notice if it is sharp or dull, if it stings or aches or pounds. See if you can't walk your awareness gently around the edges of that pain, noticing where your body transitions into the pain, shifts from pain to no pain. And breathe.

And now let your awareness gently expand out to take in each of the physical experiences you are having right now, from the strongest to the most subtle. If you find your attention drawn in to a single sensation, see if you can't expand out from that sensation to take in the whole of your physical experience. See if you can let your attention hover there, on the whole, for just a moment.

And before you end this practice, give yourself three slow, deep breaths, returning your attention back to the whole of your bodily experience with each slow breath in.

And on your next breath, take a moment to mark this experience in your memory, to note this stance toward the present as one you can return to in any moment, before it begins to gently fade away.

And breathe. And whenever you're ready, open your eyes.

What did you notice during the practice? Was your awareness scattered? Did your awareness get stuck? Were some parts easier than others? Did the practice change for you over its course? Did it remind you of anything? What else came up during the practice?

Take a moment to jot down some of the things you noticed. Try not to think too hard about making sense of your experience. See if you can't just let your thoughts flow into words.

Take a moment to read over what you've written. Now see if you can't let go of these words for now. You'll have plenty of time to wonder about how they fit and what they mean later.

If you're like most people who struggle with body image, this first part of the practice was pretty new, and it may have been pretty difficult. If you had a particularly difficult time, you might take a break and take some time to repeat the practice before moving on. Just like any other kind of skill, you will likely notice it coming more easily with each practice.

And as difficult as the first part was, most of us find being present to our appearance far more challenging. If you're willing, you'll do this next practice in front of a full-length mirror, bringing your awareness gently to your experience of your body in the mirror, and returning when you find your awareness getting scattered or stuck.

And it's going to be hard. Just like it's hard when you're trying to go about your life and you can't seem to get your head in the game. What if moving through this practice of turning and returning to your image in the mirror was practice for bringing your awareness back to the life you care about? If you're following along on the audio files that came with this book, please play track 6 at this time.

PRACTICE: Returning to the Body, Part II

Find a position a couple of feet in front of the mirror, seated or standing, where you can see most of your body.

Let your eyes come to rest upon your own eyes. Take three deep, slow breaths. As you pull the air gently into your body, and as you gently push the air out, notice the black of your pupils, and the colors that surround them, the curve of those colors. And breathe.

Notice the curve of your eyelids, the way they rest on your eyes. And breathe. Notice the curve of your lashes pushing away from your lids and back toward your skin. And breathe.

Take a moment now to broaden your awareness to the whole of your face. Notice the frame of your face—your hairline around to your jaw. Let the details of your face fill in. Notice the curves of your forehead, your cheeks, your chin, your nose, and your eyebrows. Notice the hollows that surround them. And finally let your attention come to rest on the peaks of your lips nestled there between your nose and your chin. And breathe.

And on your next breath, guide your attention down your neck and out into your shoulders. Notice the slopes that connect your arms to the rest of your body. And breathe.

Now gently let your attention flow down your arms, noticing the lines and curves that make up your arms, flesh around bone. Let your fingers spread wide as you notice each individual finger before guiding your attention back up your arms and around your shoulders. And breathe.

Take a moment to notice the movement in your chest and belly as you breathe. Watch them rise and fall as your breath flows in and out. Let your attention trace the sides of your body, noting your edges, the place where you stop. And breathe.

And on your next breath, wrap your awareness gently along your hips, around your bottom, under and back around. And breathe.

And gently, gently guide your attention along your thighs from the inside around the front and the sides of your thighs. And breathe.

And as you breathe, gently let your attention come to rest on your knees. Notice the way they interrupt your legs, transitioning from thigh to shin. And breathe.

Take a moment now to let your awareness flow down your leg along the shinbone. Let yourself notice your calf muscle spreading behind the bone, the curve it brings to your leg. And breathe.

Now gently shift your attention into your ankles. See if you can't trace the bones that protrude to allow your ankles to bend and twist. And breathe.

Let your attention drift along the tops of your feet. Take a moment now to shift your attention into your toes, one by one, from the smallest toe to the largest toe. And breathe.

With your final three breaths, let your eyes come to rest again on your eyes, but this time, see if you can't expand your awareness out to take in the whole of your visual experience of yourself right now. From the very tips of your toes to the very top of your head, take a moment to be still and see yourself. And whenever you're ready, continue reading.

Take a moment to jot down some of the things you noticed. Again, try not to think too hard about making sense of your experience; simply write what comes to you.

If you gave this second part a try, congratulations. Even if it took a few tries to get going, it likely took great courage. If you haven't gotten all the way through, it may be worth repeating the practice until you do. Of course, it's not that what shows up for you won't be upsetting. It's simply that with each practice, you'll get better and better at noticing when you become scattered or stuck, and returning to the present.

The next step is to bring all that practice to bear in your life.

Challenge and Commitment: Back to Life

Throughout this chapter, you've been reminded that practicing being present through body awareness is not for nothing. It's about learning to be present for the things that are most meaningful to you. The problem is, of course, that the situations in which body awareness would make the most meaningful difference in your life are often the ones that are most challenging. It's worth taking a moment to notice what exactly these challenges are for you.

Noticing Challenging Contexts for Body Awareness

By now, you've actually probably got a good idea of what these situations would be. These might be situations in which you lose all touch with what your body feels like or looks like right there in the moment. Or those situations in which you can't seem to pull your mind away from some feeling in or image of your body.

PRACTICE: Meaningful Challenges

Take a moment and list five situations in your life that are both meaningful to you and likely to get your awareness scattered or stuck.

Now write two numbers between 1 and 10 next to each situation, representing how meaningful (M) and how challenging (C) that situation is to you, with 10 indicating that the situation is one of the most meaningful or challenging you've experienced and 1 indicating that the situation is one of the least meaningful or challenging you've experienced.

Now, for each of the five situations, add the two numbers together. List the situations again, this time in order from that with the lowest sum (M+C) to the highest.

Give yourself a slow, deep breath. Then slowly read each situation on your list, taking three breaths on each before moving on to

65

the next. And as you breathe, imagine yourself in that situation, breathing all that you struggle with in and out.

Valued Commitment: Body Awareness Out in Your World

As you can imagine, none of this, no matter how much you put into it, will make any difference unless you extend this practice out into your life. You've gotten this far with this book because you had the sense that this stuff could help you move toward the things you really value. It's up to you to make sure the hard work you're doing doesn't stay between you and our book. So now, using your last list as a guide, we invite you to make three small commitments to practice body awareness out in your world.

Take a look at the first or second situation you wrote down, the ones with the lowest numbers, and ask yourself when you might experience this situation within the next two or three days. Then think back to the practices you did. Look back at your notes if you need to. What might be some aspect of your body experience (from the outside in or the inside out) that you'd be willing to use to bring yourself back into the present in that situation? For example, you might commit to noticing the way your shoes feel on your feet when you start to get distracted in class or a meeting. You might commit to noticing the way it feels to breathe when you find yourself worrying during a conversation. You might commit to noticing the colors in your eyes for the length of five breaths when you get stuck getting dressed tomorrow.

On a fresh page, write the numbers 1 through 3 with enough space for you to record a commitment for each. Start by writing "I commit to…" next to each number. Your first commitment should be something near the top of your ranked list, something you could do today or tomorrow. Once you have your first commitment, work your way down your list, making two more commitments of the same nature, of increasing meaning and challenge. Your second commitment might be something from the middle of the list that would take three or four days to complete. Give yourself a week to finish the last commitment.

When you have all three commitments written down, take a deep breath. If you're like most people, this is the hardest part. Your intention is recorded. Your commitment is made. The path is wide open for you to begin practicing something that is somehow simple but not at all easy. If you want to be really bold, you might consider sharing these commitments with someone you love.

And now, we would ask just a few more things of you. First, don't leave this last piece behind. Make a mark next to each commitment when you complete it, and give it another go if you set out and don't get there. Second, be kind to yourself as you step into your life practicing body awareness. Notice your inclination to shame yourself or to aim low. You're not going to learn something new like being present by bullying yourself into it. And it's not worth learning anything new if it's not in service of your values. And third, breathe. When all else fails, breathing, and noticing the experience of breathing, can often bring you back into your skin.

4 More than Words: Seeing Beyond Your Thoughts

"Thank you all for coming," Mark says as he struts through the door with his arms bowed out as if they can't lie at his sides. He notices his face starting to tingle as he realizes that he may pass out if he doesn't exhale the air he's been holding in his chest since he approached the hallway. Mark exhales as quickly as he can and sucks more air right back in, sticking his chest out even farther than before. "Does anyone remember where we left off last time?" he asks, hoping that someone actually paid attention during the last lecture he gave. Silence. He pulls his face into a scowl as he feels it start to turn red. "Anyone?" he barks as he notices a few students snickering in the back. He tries to breathe deeply, to stand up straight, and gasps several times as realizes with horror that he seems to be shrinking. It's as if his very attractive, very expensive coat is swallowing him. Mark stares blankly at his room full of students, masking the desperate resentment he feels rising from his gut. "The bombing of Hiroshima, sir." Mark is suddenly back in the classroom, noticing again that he needs to exhale.

Congratulations. If you've been working through this book the way we've suggested, you just spent a week noticing when you are not present and shifting yourself back into your skin. This was undoubtedly difficult. If you are feeling a little guilt crawling up because you didn't come back to your commitments or didn't do them as well as you could, consider hanging out there for another chunk of time. Give yourself another week. Or two. Even time you spend struggling is valuable if you notice yourself struggling and come back to what really matters here.

One of the things you might have noticed as you watched your awareness shift and practiced bringing it back into your skin is that sometimes, when your awareness gets stuck, the thing that it's stuck on seems to completely take over. Your awareness lands lightly on some thought, some concern or feeling, and suddenly, it's as if that aspect of your experience seems to grow and grow until there's no room for anything else. You might realize in the middle of a meeting that you have no idea if you put a paper you need in your bag, and suddenly the rest of your experience is lost. Your thoughts about what's going on in the moment slip away. You're no longer wondering if the presenter is right, or noticing that you're a little cold, or even laughing silently at a joke you heard the evening before. Suddenly all that exists is that paper, all the places it could be, and all the ways you might handle it if it's gone. Everything else seems somehow distant.

How It Goes: Thoughts as Lenses

In the psychological flexibility model, the tendency of thoughts to take over is called *fusion*. It turns out that we humans are very good at getting fused to all kinds of things that come up in our experience. For most of us, fusion happens over and over throughout any given day. And most of the time, the kinds of experiences we get fused with are not the kinds of things that are easily reconciled. Fused thoughts are not ones we can think our way out of, like figuring out a sum or how to spell a word. In fact, often the more we try to think them away, the further we get from getting them sorted out and moving on. Until they are reconciled, however—until you find that paper or fill out that suit—your world is limited to what you can see *through* that experience. In this way, fused thoughts come to act as lenses: everything we see, hear, feel, or remember is filtered through that fused thought.

Take a moment and call to mind the last time you felt strongly that you were *right* about something. Maybe you got a speeding ticket or argued with a friend or had to pay a late fee on a bill. Something crummy happened and you walked away feeling like you were *right* and somebody or something out in the world was doing wrong. Call to mind what it was like experiencing your world through the lens of being right yet being wronged. Watch yourself going the places you go, being with the people you know. Not only were you likely struggling to really be present, but the things you *did* notice or engage with probably fed right into your fusion. Most of your experiences probably either made you feel more right, more wronged, or both.

When the Lenses Show Up

When it comes to fusion, all thoughts are not created equal. Certain kinds of thoughts are easier to fuse with. In fact, certain kinds of thoughts are hard to even have without fusing to them. Psychologists have long noticed that thoughts that present some kind of absolute certainty or rule are not a great fit for the world. The world isn't obviously split into rights and wrongs, cans and can'ts, or shoulds and shouldn'ts. People aren't simply good or bad.

Even life changes like moving, or breaking up, or getting a new car aren't entirely good or entirely bad.

So rules about the way the world is or the way it should be tend to cause problems for us. The problem with these thoughts isn't that we have them, though. Humans can't help but try to fit the world into absolutes. We can't help but make rules to try to get us through the world with a little more ease. The problem with these thoughts is that when they come, we tend to fuse with them. We take them on as lenses and suddenly less of our world is available to us.

Take a moment and read over these incomplete statements slowly, letting your mind complete them as you reach each blank.

People shouldn't _____.

I should really _____.

No matter how hard I try, I can't seem to _____.

It's wrong for me to _____.

No one ever _____.

What did you notice? If you're like most people, your mind did what it does automatically and without your permission or input. It simply completed the statements. Your mind filled in the blanks.

Now take just that first one, this time jotting down what shows up:

People shouldn't _____.

Got it? Now read it again, jotting down what shows up this time. Read it two or three more times, jotting down what shows up each time. Now four or five more.

Did your mind ever have any trouble completing the statement? If you're like most people, the answer is no. In fact, you could probably read just that phrase forty times and your mind could complete it forty different ways. A few of the completed statements would be unfamiliar thoughts that you don't even really recognize as your own. Some of them would be thoughts that come up for you but that you don't really believe. Some of the thoughts that would come up would be strikingly familiar. It's worth noticing the thoughts you recognize and really believe when they come up. While we have the ability to fuse with any thought, most of us have a few that we regularly let take over.

Your Lenses

We all have certain thoughts we tend to fuse with over and over again. This is sort of like having a little box of lenses we whip out when things get tough. Something shifts in our world that we don't like and we start seeing the world a certain way. As much as they affect our experiences, though, we are often completely unaware that these lenses are even there. Have you ever suddenly realized the reason it looked so dark so early in the evening was that you were still wearing your sunglasses? Just like you only notice your sunglasses for a few seconds after putting them on, you simply take your experience as the way the world is. It isn't until something really doesn't make sense that you start to question it.

It's worth taking a moment to examine the lenses you carry. Noticing the kinds of thoughts you tend to fuse with is the first step to being able to experience your world fully without any one thought taking over. If you're following along on the audio files that came with this book, please play track 7 at this time.

PRACTICE: Seeing Your Lenses

Take a look at your notes from the last exercise in chapter 3, "Meaningful Challenges." You should see a list of five situations in your life that are both meaningful to you and hard to stay present in. Use this list to make a new list on a new page, this time of three meaningful situations you encounter in your life. They can be three from the list, or if others seem more important now, it can be a new list altogether. Leave ten to fifteen lines after each situation in the list.

Take a moment to familiarize yourself with the situations so you can use them in an eyes-closed exercise. Don't spend too much time trying to memorize them, though. If you forget, you can always peek.

Let your eyes fall closed, and breathe. Take three slow, deep breaths to recognize what it feels like to breathe. Imagine that with each breath, you can feel yourself sinking more and more firmly into your skin, right now. And breathe.

See if you can't create, with your breath, a path back to the present, back into your skin. And breathe.

As you feel yourself settle, call to mind the first situation on your list. Call this situation up, as if you could watch glimpses of it at different times, like you would a trailer for a movie. Make room for glimpses of times when you made the most of this mean-ingful situation in your life and for glimpses of times you didn't. And breathe.

On your next breath, settle on a time when this situation didn't go like you wanted, a time when you weren't the person you want to be there. Imagine you could pour yourself into your skin in that moment, seeing the world through your eyes in that moment, feeling all the things that were swirling within you. And breathe.

Take a few moments to notice what kinds of thoughts, feelings, and memories show up for you there. When you find yourself getting scattered or stuck, take a deep breath and allow the sensations of your breath to guide you back to the present and to this image of you in a challenging, yet meaningful situation. And breathe.

When you're ready, open your eyes and jot down a few notes on the kinds of thoughts that showed up. If you find it hard to wrap words around your experience, see if you can't let it go and record a few words—just enough writing that you'll know what you meant

when you read it again. Move slowly through this process of record-
ing the thoughts that show up, including the most obvious thoughts
as well as some of those thoughts that are better defended. And
breathe, letting your eyes fall gently closed when you've written
what was there to write, and moving on to the second situation in
your list.

Call up the other two situations in this way—first letting
different times this situation came up tumble through your mind,
then settling on one example of a time when you found yourself
struggling to contact what is meaningful to you in this situation.
Again, slip yourself into your own skin in that moment and notice
what thoughts show up.

When you've called up each of your three situations and have a
few thoughts written down for each, take a few moments to breathe
yourself back into the now before moving on.

Now take a few moments to look over your list. What kinds of
thoughts do you get fused with in these vulnerable moments that
are both meaningful and challenging? What kind of lenses do you
tend to wear when things get tough? How do your lenses change in
different situations? Is there something similar about the kinds of
lenses you take on, regardless of the situation?

Put a star by any of the thoughts you wrote down that seem like
things that you get fused with a lot, in many different situations.
Now, I want you to do something that may seem a little strange.
Near each sentence you starred, write down a sentence that means
the opposite. For example, if you wrote, "You can't trust anybody,"
write near it, "You can trust anyone." If you wrote, "I am selfish,"
write, "I am selfless and giving." If you wrote, "I am lazy," write, "I
am hardworking." Don't rush through the writing. See if you can't
sort of try the statement on as you write it. Say it to yourself as if
you were encouraging a friend to see a different point of view.

When you have the second sentence written, read your original
sentence and its opposite through, back and forth, a couple of
times. What do you notice as you read through them? What's it like

to read through your opposite sentence? What does your mind do there? If the first brings discomfort and fusion, does the second bring relief? Freedom? Peace?

For most folks, the answer is no—there's no relief in telling yourself the opposite. And there's a good reason why. Our fused thoughts show up as being totally one-sided. Our minds, though, are constantly comparing and evaluating the sense we are making of the world. Even as you read these words on this page, you're mentally comparing them to things you know and the experiences you've had. *Wait, is that true? I guess it sort of is. Oh, I see, it's like this. Yes, that works. Wait, I'm not sure about this here. I learned it a little differently.*

This is exactly what most people notice when they read through their opposite statement. They barely get through it before their minds are busy with *Well, no, that's not really...* or *Yeah right, you wish...* or *Well, that's true, but only in the sense that...* When you tell yourself the opposite of a fused thought, you're not shedding that lens, you're just flipping it around and looking through it again. And things seem strange when they're backwards. Fusion is not about negative or positive thoughts. Positive thoughts are just as likely to dominate as negative thoughts are, and thoughts don't zero out the way sums do. Adding a positive to a negative doesn't make it go away. In fact, the positive and the negative are different in what they say but not really different in how they affect us. It seems the fused thought and its opposite are just two sides of the same lens.

Fusion and Struggles with Body Image

We think that fusion is a major part of body image struggles. For one, those of us who struggle with body image are way more likely to get fused when we're feeling bad about our bodies. You may find you are most fused, most likely to put on those lenses, when you feel your appearance might be judged. You see someone you haven't seen in a long time. You give a presentation at work or school. You're being fitted for a wedding you're in. You're meeting someone new. You see three other applicants in the waiting room before a job interview. Someone is taking your picture. And suddenly the world is dropping away and those familiar thoughts start to take over. Take a moment to look back at your notes from the last practice. How many of the situations you wrote down include some aspect of your appearance being evaluated? And now–how many of the situations you didn't dare write down include some aspect of your appearance being evaluated?

For some of us, our body lenses are at the ready, no matter what the situation. Maybe for you, hard situations always seem to turn into struggles with your body. Maybe you're sad or stressed or worried about something else altogether, but somehow it always seems to feed into feeling ugly or fat or deformed. You ask a question and no one answers. You wake up on the wrong side of the bed. A waiter charges your credit card twice. A friend lets you down. You lose your keys. You hurt someone's feelings. Something hard happens in the world, and somehow if feels like all that hurt inside is evident on the outside. As if anyone looking at you would certainly see.

Take a moment to look at the list of fused thoughts you wrote. Circle any of the thoughts you wrote down that are about the body. Now notice the body thoughts you didn't write down—the ones you don't say out loud, the ones you work so hard to push away. If you're willing, add those to your list. And breathe.

Costs of the Struggle with Body Thoughts

We all have moments of body fusion, when our experience of the body takes over. And in those moments, your experience of your body becomes your experience of the world. The things most obvious or engaging there are the threats, the things that help you monitor threats, and sources of relief or protection. You might get lost in thoughts about how you look, what others must think, or how you could fix your appearance. You might not even notice a person you really like and are just getting to know because you're unable to stop tracking and trying to hide from someone you think always looks perfect. You might think about the situation with regret later, noticing how small your world got that day.

Take a moment and read over the body thoughts you wrote down. If you're willing, go through your body thoughts slowly, one at a time. Take a moment with each of them, imagining the different situations in your life in which it takes over. Notice how it matters more in some situations than others. See if it's not the case that the more important it feels that body thoughts not interfere in a certain situation, the more they do. For this next practice, choose a situation in which it feels important that body thoughts not interfere. If you're following along with the audio, advance to track 8.

PRACTICE: Lost Behind Lenses

Take a deep breath and let your eyes close slowly. Take a moment to feel what it's like to breathe, drawing air in and out of your body. See if you can't feel your awareness settling more and more into this moment with each breath. And breathe.

On your next breath, call to mind a relationship, or an aspiration, or an activity in your life with which you really hate for body thoughts to interfere. Maybe it's when you have to talk in front of people. Maybe it's when you're buying clothes. Maybe it's at the beach or the gym. Maybe it's around your family or a certain group of friends. Maybe it's that moment when you realize someone wants to hug or hold or touch you.

If you find yourself struggling with which situation to use or to recall any situation at all, give yourself a full breath, imagining that, on your exhale, that flurry of activity in your mind has more and more room to simply settle. And breathe.

And let yourself see a specific time when this situation was changed by your body thoughts and the way they affect you. Pause the memory and take a full breath. If you're wanting to turn away from this memory, imagine that staying with it just a little longer could give you strength for the next time something like this comes up. Breathe, letting your breath bring you back each time your awareness starts to become scattered or stuck.

And as you breathe, let the tiny details fill in:
where you were,
who (if anyone) was there with you,
what you were doing,
the look on your face,
how you held your body.

If there are details you can't muster up, make them up. And breathe.

On your next breath, lift the pause and let the memory gradually unfold before you. Notice the moment when fusion took hold. See if you can't tell, from the outside, just when the lenses sank over your eyes. Watch how your face changes in the instant the lenses come down, the way you hold yourself. See if you can't see in your eyes how they stop seeing.

And now, notice how your world changed in that moment when the lenses came down. Were you still hearing? Still seeing? Still tasting and smelling? Were you still feeling all there was to feel?

Notice how your behavior changed as the world faded. See if you can't pick out the moment when you lost contact with what it was you were trying to do in that situation. Watch where your fusion took you. And breathe.

And as you breathe, see if you can't let yourself wonder: What possibilities and opportunities fell away as the world became more and more hidden behind thoughts about your body? What could have been? Take a moment to notice the opportunity lost. And on your next breath, let your eyes come open.

What kinds of things do you notice were lost to you once fusion took over?

We assume that having a fuller experience of your world is a good thing. But not only that—just as with being present, we assume that some of that stuff that slips away, that stuff you lose, is stuff that really matters to you or could matter to you. You lose a peaceful moment with someone you care about. You lose a look a loved one gives that says, "You hurt my feelings." You lose the praise your boss is trying to give you for a job well done. You lose something pretty or funny or fun.

And in those moments of loss, fusion can rob you of opportunities, small and great, to live the life you want. We think it's worth practicing an alternative. Not because we say so, but because you deserve every moment your life has to offer.

An Alternative: Seeing Your Thoughts and Beyond

This idea that thoughts can take over your world and limit your behavior is not new. Just as when you say, "Every time I move my arm it hurts," somebody says, "Well, don't move," there's always been this idea that if these thoughts interfere with your life, you should stop thinking them. This is not, however, the easiest thing to do. Have you ever tried *not* to think about something?

Take a moment right here and try this out. Grab a timer and set it for one minute. Once you've set it your only job is, for the whole minute, to not think about a red ball. And when you do think about the red ball, just make a small mark in your notebook.

Now count up your marks. How many times did the red ball come up for you? Two? Six? Ten? Twenty? For most people, it's between six and ten. Maybe you start by reciting the Happy Birthday song or solving addition problems in your head. You might think, *A B C D E F... Hey, this isn't so bad. I haven't thought about the red ball once!* But then, of course, there it is. Typically when we are trying not to think something, we very frequently—every ten seconds or so—check to see if we are thinking about it. And that checking in involves (you guessed it) thinking about the very thing we're trying not to think about. And that's just in one minute! If we stick with six, that's 360 an hour. Or more than five thousand during one day waking. Just not thinking about something is not an easy task. In fact, we tend to think about something more when we're trying not to than when we just let what comes come!

And not just that. Every time we think about it, new paths to the thought are formed. Whatever was happening just before we thought about it—whatever we saw or smelled or thought or remembered—suddenly that's a reminder for the very thought we were trying to not think! If you sang "Happy Birthday" to not think of the red ball, you're more likely to think of a red ball at the next birthday party you attend.

Now, that's just a red ball. Presumably you don't have any strong feelings or meaning connected to red balls. But what if the thing you're trying hard not to think about feels terribly important? What if the thought you're trying to keep at bay is, essentially, how you see yourself? Call to mind a part of your body that you wish looked different. Now take a minute and try not to think about it. Set your timer for thirty seconds this time and mark how many times you thought about the forbidden body part.

Not much better, is it? In fact, for many, it's much, much worse.

A more involved way we try to get rid of thoughts is by thinking an opposite thought or thinking about evidence that the thought isn't true. Recall earlier in the chapter when you wrote down fused thoughts and their opposites. Take a moment and call to mind a part of your body that you wish looked different. Notice what thoughts come up: My _____ *is so* _____. You might jot a couple down. Now, go one by one through each thought you wrote down about your body, and, as you read the thought, simply think its opposite. If you noticed, *My belly is so fat,* think My *belly is so thin.* Write down what shows up. Now take that same thought, except instead of thinking the opposite, think of a slight change that might make it easier to bear. If your thought was *My belly is fat*, you might think, *I could use some more crunches*, or *But my arms are toned*, or *It's really just right for my body.*

What do you notice? What happened as you told yourself you were good-looking or your belly was flat or your blemishes weren't noticeable? Most of us are very able to think the opposite thoughts or to come up with evidence that our fused thoughts are wrong. The challenge is not in generating the conflicting thoughts, but in what happens afterward. Just because you're generating new thoughts on purpose doesn't mean your mind isn't commenting on every new thought you come up with.

It might go something like this:

You: My thighs are shapely.

Your mind: Flabby is more like it.

You: Lots of men are attractive and bald.

Your mind: You weren't that good-looking when you had hair.

You: My skin just needs more attention.

Your mind: Like some sort of sandblaster.

You: I can still be kind and hardworking.

Your mind: You better be kind and hardworking when you look like this.

You: With the right outfit, no one will notice.

Your mind: But you'll always know. You'll never be comfortable.

You: I'm long and slender.

Your mind: So are preteen boys.

Even though it makes intellectual sense, trying to add thoughts that conflict logically with thoughts that are already there isn't the best way to stop fusion. First, even when we're able to flip a lens and look through it the opposite way, our world is still being filtered through that lens. And when seeing through any lens (whether it feels good or bad), we're not experiencing the world fully. More than that, though, the deal with thoughts seems to be that you can only add, never take away. And while making room for other thoughts to show up could get you to a point where that fused thought isn't taking up all the space, it can also help fusion grow. Especially if you're adding thoughts to try to get rid of the first one. It's just like what happens when we're trying not to think about something: we tend to constantly go back and check if that first thought is still there.

What if every time we think of a new thought and then check for the old, fused thought, those two thoughts become linked? What if telling yourself you're good-looking every time you feel ugly means that next time you feel good-looking, feeling ugly will be right alongside it, quicker and stronger every time? Not only does doing all that back and forth in our minds give us more practice with fusing with that thought, but while we're doing that, our world is still going, and important moments are being lost.

So what's the out? How do we get rid of those lenses once and for all? Well, here's our confession: we don't. Trying to stop thoughts, and attack thoughts, and whittle away at thoughts—all of these tactics make perfect sense. It's no wonder that this is how we typically handle thoughts that tend to take over. But just because it makes sense doesn't mean it works like we would expect.

The thing most people never even consider is this: What if you don't need a way out? What if you don't need the lenses to fall away for you to be able to experience your life all the way? What if all you need is a little bit of room?

Imagine that our thoughts are less like lenses and more like messages—an e-mail, a text message, or a little hand-scrawled note. Suppose someone sent you a message. And you were pretty sure it was important, so when your phone buzzed or you found the note on your door, it grabbed your awareness. But every time you went to look at the message, you put it right up to your eyes like it was a lens—something to look through instead of at. Take a moment and try this out. Grab your phone or tablet, open a text message or an e-mail, and hold it just in front of your eyes. Or grab a sticky note or a notebook and hold it right there in front of your face. Hold it two inches from your eyes. What do you see?

First, what do you see of the world? Well, pretty much just the words you're holding in front of you, right? Imagine you were trying to write an e-mail, or feed a pet, or repair something, or have a conversation with someone you love. How effective would you be with this message smashed right up against your face? Probably not very.

And not only that.

How well would you be able to read the message itself? Grab a message again and hold it two inches from your eyes. You'll be lucky to make out any words at all. Now suppose that this message is about something that really matters to you. It's about what the next step is for an important project or what needs to happen next in a precious relationship. You might make out one or two words and find yourself trying frantically to guess what's going on. And there you are, struggling to receive a message with it smashed up against your face.

So you've got this important message coming at you, and you can't see a word of it or *anything else* because of the way you're holding it. What's the only thing to do? If you want to receive the message, if you want to be able to be in your world, what do you have to do?

What if fusion is like this? It's not what the words say that's problematic; it's the way we tend to hold them right up against us. And what if the only action that makes any sense when we notice we've got something smashed up against our faces is to move it out a little to where we can see it? To get some space between it and us, so it can be there along with everything else? In the psychological flexibility model, we call this *defusion*, and the goal is to hold our thoughts in such a way that we can see what they are telling us, decide how and if they are important, and see the world around us so we can choose how to respond.

And this takes practice. We are so used to treating thoughts as lenses instead of as just another part of our experience. Most of us don't really realize that it could be any other way. Next, we'll take a few moments to practice noticing defusing from body thoughts when they take over. If you're following along on the audio files that came with this book, please play track 9 at this time.

PRACTICE: Seeing Beyond Body Image

Let your eyes fall gently closed, feeling yourself settle into your skin more and more as your visual world disappears. And when your eyes are completely closed, take a moment to just breathe, in and out. Notice what it's like to breathe—to take air into your body— and to release. And breathe.

On your next breath, call to mind a situation in your life in which you suffer because of the way your body thoughts take over. If you want to be really bold, you might pick something even more difficult for you than the situation you chose in the last practice. A place where you're a little more vulnerable, or a situation involving someone precious. Let your mind settle on one important aspect of your life in which body fusion is interfering. And breathe.

And let it be that, with your next breath, on your next glance, you suddenly open your eyes before a mirror where you are preparing to step into that hard situation. Maybe you're getting dressed and examining how you look. Maybe you've snuck away for the bathroom before things get difficult in a social situation, and you happen to catch your reflection in the mirror on your way out. Maybe you've positioned yourself in front of the mirror to talk your-

self into what you're about to do. As you face yourself in the mirror, see if you can't feel the tension that comes with preparing for something significant. And breathe.

Take a moment here to breathe yourself into your body. What does it feel like inside your skin right now? And as you breathe, watch your chest rise and fall in the mirror. And as you feel your feet on the ground, see your feet on the ground in the mirror. And as you feel your clothes on your skin, see your clothes hug and hang against your skin. And breathe.

Take a moment to call to mind once more that tough but important thing you're about to walk into. To notice what's at stake. And breathe. And as you breathe, notice the flurry of activity that's happening in your mind as you watch yourself settle into your skin in the mirror. Notice those moments when you get scattered or stuck, and breathe yourself back into your body. See if you can't, with each breath, make a little more room for all those thoughts to be there, bouncing about behind your eyes. And breathe.

And, in the space your breath is creating, see if you notice the judgments your mind makes about your body. Let your eyes rest on each of the parts of your body most troublesome to you, one at a time. And as your eyes come to rest on that part of your body, hear what it is that your mind says is wrong with it. And breathe.

And if you find yourself wanting to turn away from your reflection or end the exercise, let it be that sticking with yourself in this moment could be offering you some strength when all this comes up out in the world. And breathe.

On your next breath, realize that not only can you hear the thoughts your mind has about your body, but that you can see them, too. Let it be that as a judgment about your body comes up, it gradually becomes visible in the mirror, just in front of that part of you. Maybe your judgments take the shape of words, labels like "ugly," "disgusting," "deformed," or "fat." Maybe they show up as objects or substances with color and shape and form. Let your-

self watch as your thoughts become visible, some showing up then fading away, others showing up and sticking around, maybe even growing bigger and bigger the longer they're there. And breathe.

And, as you breathe, notice that your reflection becomes more and more hidden behind your body thoughts. Maybe lots of different ones on the same theme. Maybe one thought that's grown so big, it's completely taken over. Notice more and more gather in the mirror, blocking out your body. And breathe.

And give yourself a slow breath and let it be that you could reach out into the mirror and pull just one of those body thoughts from it, out of the mirror and into the space around you. Imagine you could hold it in your hand. Maybe it has a temperature, a texture. Maybe a weight. Take a few breaths to see it, feel it there, in your hand. Consider it, like you might an interesting stone you'd come across.

On your next breath, imagine that you could gently set that hard thought back into the mirror. Watch it fade slowly away, and notice as your reflection becomes increasingly visible. And breathe, watching and feeling yourself in your body as you breathe.

Let yourself notice the body thoughts showing up in the mirror. Again, pick one to draw gently from the mirror and into your hand. And breathe. And take a few moments to study the thought in your hand, the way it looks and feels there, before gently placing it back into the mirror, where you watch it fade away. Notice what parts of your reflection are visible now, and what parts remain hidden. And breathe, watching and feeling your breath enter and leave your body.

Take a few moments now to pull three more difficult thoughts from the mirror, one at a time, considering each carefully before replacing them in the mirror and watching them fade away. And breathe, each time, letting your breath settle you deeper into your skin, while making more and more room for your experiences to gather.

Give yourself three final breaths, and open your eyes.

Take a moment to sketch out what you saw in the mirror in this practice. First draw the mirror, and write your first name (or what people call you) above it. Then sketch your shape in the mirror. Just a silhouette is fine. Add as many or as few details as you want. As you draw, notice the urge to draw yourself a certain way. To narrow your waist and hips a little, include more hair than you have, or round out muscles you wish you had. Take a deep breath and see if you can't let go of that urge and draw as close to your shape as you can. Next draw some of the thoughts you saw in the mirror before you pulled them away. After you draw each one, close your eyes briefly and see that image fade into the mirror, your reflection revealed behind it. And keep breathing.

When you're finished, put this drawing in a place where you can come back to it, adding new things that come up as you move through the rest of this book. Before moving on, you might try revisiting this exercise in front of a real mirror. Close your eyes and see thoughts show up in the mirror each time you feel yourself getting fused. Then take a moment to pull them from the mirror and consider them before letting them fade away and opening your eyes to your reflection.

In our next section, we'll talk about how to practice defusion out in the world.

Challenge and Commitment: When Thoughts Save You

Just like any of the four opportunities for change, body defusion is something that has to be practiced—and not just with your eyes closed or when you're in front of the mirror. Practice only means something because of the game. Setting aside time to practice defusion only means something because of the life you're trying to live that fusion is interfering with. If an athlete can only catch the ball in practice, it's meaningless. If you can only defuse from body thoughts in a scripted exercise, it's meaningless. The goal is to build the skill so that you can use it when you need it the most. Of course, though, when you most need it is when it is most challenging.

Noticing Challenging Contexts for Body Defusion

Look back over some of the work you've done in this chapter. You should already have a pretty good idea of what situations, activities, or relationships are contexts in which you are way likely to get fused. If you're like most people, they're not random. For most of us, the contexts in which we get really fused are ones that have been difficult for us (or that remind us of ones that have been difficult for us).

Fusion has a job. It works, to some extent. It just has costs. See, fusion can be pretty miserable, but it often saves us from something that's not just miserable, but that also makes us vulnerable. Something that hurts much worse to expose. You can imagine fusion as this hard outer shell—this armor that covers something softer and more vulnerable.

This is probably easiest to get if you think about the feelings that come with hard thoughts. Think about times you've been angry instead of sad, or annoyed instead of hurt. Times when you've been exasperated instead of lost, or disgusted instead of disappointed. Notice how easily these feelings take over, how hard it is for anything else to get through. When you're feeling disgusted or exasperated, often that's all you're feeling. Notice the rigidity they bring. It's like there is literally no room for anything else to be there.

Now call to mind times when the anger dissipated or someone broke through the annoyance. What else was there to be felt now that there was space inside you? What was hidden underneath the fusion?

Fusion is most likely to come up in situations in which we've been hurt, because its function is to save us from being hurt again. Being disgusted with your appearance hurts less than letting the disappointment of what you see in the mirror rise up inside you. It's like Mark growing slowly infuriated with his class as a sort of desperate shame grew within him; in that same way, fusion saves us sometimes. Except that sometimes the things it saves us from are things that really matter to us. What if the areas where we're vulnerable are connected to the things we care about most? After all, we wouldn't bother to wrap something in armor unless it was precious and deserved to be protected.

In those moments when you take a fused thought and hold it out where you can experience it clearly, it's worth asking yourself, *If I peeled back the layers of this, what might lie underneath?* or *What vulnerability is this fusion saving me from?* Take another look at the picture you drew after the last practice, and let yourself wonder: What was left when all the fusion dissipated? What would be left if you stopped hating your body, even for just a moment? If you know, it might be worth jotting down a few words. If you don't know, mark this as something to revisit.

Valued Commitment: Body Defusion Out in Your World

Before you move on, the last challenge is to extend this practice out into your life. Just as we did in the last chapter, we invite you to make three small commitments to practice body defusion out in your world in a way that might move you toward your values. Each commitment should be a little harder than the last and a little more meaningful, so you'll give yourself a little more time to finish each commitment up.

Start by taking a look back at the work you did in this chapter. Notice the situations in which fusion comes up, as well as the kinds of thoughts you tend to get fused with. Be open to things coming up that you might not have written down before. Feel free to add to your notes if what you have written down feels incomplete or off.

When you feel you've got a sense of your struggle, number a fresh page 1 through 3 with a few blank lines after each number. Now imagine the next week rolling out in front of you. What do you have going on? Where are you going? Who are you likely to encounter? What kinds of activities are you likely to engage in? Of the different places you'll go and issues you'll run into, where might body fusion try to get in your way in the next seven days? What thoughts and feelings are likely to come up there? But not just that: What's going to be important to you in the next seven days or so? Where might you have the opportunity to take a step toward your valued life? What might that step look like?

Next to your number 1, write down your first defusion commitment. This one should be something relatively simple that you could do in a couple of days. Be specific about the situation in which you'll practice defusion, what thoughts and feelings you'll be defusing from, and what you'll do to defuse. It could start with something like *When I'm dressing for work, and I have the thought that my face is deformed...* or *When I'm at the sales meeting, and I can't shake the thought that I'm balding...* or *When I'm cuddling with my boyfriend, and I keep having the thought that he's going to touch my disgusting thigh...* The more specific you are with your commitment, the better. Yet—be ready to change it up if another opportunity comes up.

Be creative with your actual body defusion technique. Anything that acknowledges and gives you some space from the body thought will help you defuse. You can practice noticing a fused thought as an object or a word like we did in the last exercise, then shifting your attention back out to the whole of your experience. You can practice hearing your thoughts like songs or a radio broadcast. You might consider having a friend on call to hear you express fused body thoughts without having to do or say anything about it. For example, you could text a friend, "I'm having the thought that I'm hideous and no one will ever love me," and have him or her simply receive the text without even responding to what you're saying. Your friend might text nothing back, or text, "Ouch. That's terrible." But you'd have asked the person ahead of time not to text something like "No, you're not! I love you!"

After you've got your first commitment down in the format described, push yourself to think of slightly more difficult things for both of the next two commitments. Maybe you push yourself a little harder and act a little bolder in what you actually do to defuse. Maybe you pick harder, scarier thoughts to defuse from. The second commitment should be something you'll do in four or five days, and the third commitment should be something that might take the whole week.

When you've got your commitments recorded, let your eyes close just briefly and notice how difficult it is to express an intention to change something. How scary it is to commit to doing something different. If you're willing to be really bold, you might consider sharing your commitments with someone you love.

Don't rush on to the next chapter. Spend some time with each of these commitments, one at a time. Notice the impact they have in your life. Mark each commitment when you've completed it. And if you find yourself not moving forward, it may be that your two-day commitment is a bigger deal than you thought. Maybe it would be a better fit for your seven-day commitment. It also may be that you stayed away from the things that are most meaningful and ended up with something that doesn't really matter enough to move on. And in those moments where it feels like trying to do something different is getting you more stuck than before, it might be worth looking at your thoughts around commitment and working on defusion there, too.

5 Opening Up: Accepting the Unacceptable

Bethany makes her way through the empty aisles of the grocery store, studying the shelves, placing items carefully in the cart, marking each item off her list, and recalculating her total. She enjoys the repetition, and it has her total attention.

"Bethany?"

A voice breaks through her focus. She is obviously surprised as she checks her watch before turning toward the voice. 5:15 a.m. Who could be here? "Wow! Susan?" she says, choking the words out as she feels her stomach start to turn. She hasn't seen her neighbor from high school in ten years, but she recognizes Susan's smile right away. *I swear she looks exactly the same. God, why is she here?* Bethany thinks, as Susan pulls her into a warm hug.

"You know, I tried to get in touch with you a few months ago, B!" Susan releases Bethany from the hug, but clutches her left arm as she continues, "I was getting some of the girls together. Let's see—Kristian came, and Ricki—oh my God, you have got to see her baby..."

Why is she here? She's never been here before. No one comes to the grocery store at 4:30 in the morning on a Saturday to catch up. I look awful. This is ridiculous. God, what is she talking about? I have got to find a mirror.

"And it's just been... well... hard, ya know? Look, I know we haven't talked in a while, but jeez, I could really use a friend with everything going on. Do you think... I mean, could I call you for coffee or something? You were always so good to me. I mean, I know you're busy... But... Would you be okay with that, though? Coffee? Maybe?" Susan's smile has wilted and her eyes are brimming with a sort of longing that seems to grow every second.

"Yeah, Susan. Sure. What are friends for?" Bethany hears her voice like it's coming from outside her body and feels grateful that some part of her knows how to end all this. "Any..." She breaks off as she suddenly notices a few baskets and picture frames in a perpendicular aisle behind Susan's head. *A mirror!* Bethany feels the relief flood in. It gives her a new strength. "Anytime—seriously." She touches Susan's hand and smiles warmly until she sees Susan blink back her tears.

"Okay then! Sorry about this. Not to be dramatic. I just... Thanks, B. I miss you. I'm sorry. I'll call!" Susan is still talking as she begins to move herself away. Bethany watches her walk away, feeling pangs of pain as she notices how completely lovely Susan looks in her leggings and sports bra. *Ugh... Like a commercial for gym clothes.*

As soon as Susan has passed out of sight, Bethany begins moving her cart with growing urgency toward the housewares section she'd noticed over Susan's shoulder. A *mirror, a mirror, a mirror.* She can feel a cold sweat breaking out on her face as she scans shelf after shelf. *Mirror, mirror, mirror.* "Ah!"

Heart pounding, Bethany walks directly up to the first full-length mirror on an aisle half-filled with them, picks one up, and sets it on the floor. She closes her eyes and fills her lungs before stepping in front of the mirror. Opening her eyes, she can see her body becoming more and more relaxed as she works her way up her body fixing this and that—straightening her waistband, smoothing her pants down her thighs, unbuttoning and rebuttoning shirt buttons, running her fingers through her hair.

There you go. Much better. We'll be ready now. We'll be all ready. Now. Let's see... cereal...

What if there are only two kinds of things? What if we can categorize all we know into just two kinds of things: experiences (our world) and behaviors (the things we do about it)? After all, everything we do is in response to some shift in our world—the world around us or the world within us. Our world shifts and our behavior shifts to better fit what is needed from one moment to the next. Our world is constantly changing, which means our behavior is in constant, dynamic flow from one moment to the next.

One of the things we touched on at the end of the last chapter was how fusion can sometimes save us from having to think or feel things that are particularly painful. You may have noticed that when you defuse and you get a more careful look at what's going on for you, often you are faced with something difficult, something you'd like to be able to get away from. With all of the experiences that flow through our awareness in any one moment, over the course of a day or a week or a month or a year, many of our experiences are things we don't like to spend much time thinking about or feeling.

And we don't respond to difficult experiences with fusion alone. Fusion often comes with all kinds of other behaviors that save us from our experiences. In fact, we could literally sort almost every single thing we do into two kinds of behaviors: those that bring us into contact with some aspect of our experience and those that take us away.

Think about the things you've done in just the past hour. Jot four or five of them down. Maybe you turned off an alarm or reminder. Maybe you turned up the volume on the radio. Maybe you denied an incoming call or skipped over an e-mail you read. Maybe you held your coworker's baby or ate a piece of pizza. Maybe you paid for some stamps at the post office.

Now think about what was going on just before you engaged in that behavior, and what was going on just after.

The alarm was ringing, and then you turned it off. Turning the alarm off brought you away from the ringing.

You saw the pizza on your plate, took a bite, and tasted delicious pizza. Taking a bite helped you make contact with the taste of the pizza.

Maybe holding the baby put you in contact with the baby's soft skin and sweet face. Maybe holding the baby brought you away from the crying the baby was doing just before.

Most of the things you did in the past hour were things you had to learn to do at some point in your life. You weren't born turning off alarms or buying stamps. You learned these behaviors according to a very simple principle: selection by consequences. Every behavior we engage in has some consequence in the world. Every behavior we engage in changes our experience in some way, if only for an instant. The consequences of a behavior, the nature of that change, determine how likely the behavior is to happen again. Some consequences make a behavior more likely to happen again. Other consequences make a behavior less likely to happen again. If you pick up a baby and it laughs, you might be more likely to pick up the baby next time. If it bursts into tears the second you pick it up, you might walk the other way when you see a stroller coming. We are constantly learning new behaviors and strengthening existing behaviors. Every time you take a bite of delicious pizza, it strengthens that behavior—makes it more likely you'll do it again. If you took a bite of pizza and got violently ill, you might not be as likely to eat pizza again even if it had been a regular thing in your life.

The consequences that make a behavior more likely either bring you into contact with something you'll work for or bring you away from something you'll work to avoid. And we humans are much better at learning to move away from things in the world than to move toward them. We are simply built for avoidance. When there's something to move away from, we are faster at learning how, we learn more ways to get away, and once we learn them, it takes a longer time to change. It's with this kind of behavior that many of our difficulties or inflexibilities arise.

How It Goes: Run, Trap, or Kill

Learning to get away from stuff, or *avoidance*, is a pretty adaptive skill. It's no wonder we learn it so well. You can imagine back in the caveman days that if there was something in the world that was threatening us, being able to get away from it meant we got to stay alive and with all our limbs intact. If there was a predator looking for lunch, for example, being able to run, trap, or kill was a real skill. The cougar would show up, and the caveman would start doing whatever he could to solve the problem. He would run away and hide. He'd trap the beast and escape unharmed. He'd face his predator and fight for his life. If the cougar showed up, the caveman would stop whatever he was doing and run, trap, or kill.

And not only that. Our cavemen ancestors learned not only to stop what they were doing and run, trap, or kill when they saw or heard a cougar, but also when something signaled a cougar—if they heard a flock of birds alight suddenly, or if they smelled blood on the air. Certain marks in the dirt or on the trees would set them to run, trap, or kill before they'd even seen the thing they were avoiding. Cougars were not only where they physically were, cougars were anywhere that signals were.

There were some slight disadvantages to all this. We'd end up running or fighting instead of other important stuff like collecting stones or carving wood. We'd set traps and limit the areas we could travel freely in. But generally, this was all worth it. The cavemen who were still collecting stones or carving wood or roaming free when the cougar attacked didn't last long enough to pass on their genes.

Escaping What We Carry: Experiential Avoidance

Avoidance is an important kind of learning that every multicellular organism in the world exhibits. There's something different about it with humans, though. We learned not only to run, trap, or kill every time we ran across a cougar, and to set to running, trapping, or killing any time the situation signaled a cougar, but we also developed ways to carry those signals with us. If one caveman saw a predator, a carcass, or some scratches on a tree, he could come back to the cave and signal the other guys to join him. And when he did, it was, for him and for them, as if the cougar were there, ready to attack. One caveman said the word and they all stopped whatever else they were doing and coordinated an effort to run or trap or kill as efficiently as possible.

It may be this very skill of creating signals for events in our world that allowed us to cooperate and survive running, trapping, or killing even when the animals were much scarier and more dangerous than ourselves. It may be that being able to make monsters present where they are not has kept the human race going strong even now that we rarely face big fangs or sharp claws or warm fur. The problem is, of course, that we don't just carry signals of things that could eat us for lunch. We carry signals of all kinds of hurts.

We try to run or trap or kill memories of a dangerous time that has long since passed. We try to run or trap or kill fears about what might come next. We try to run or trap or kill judgments about how we're doing or what's wrong with us. Anxiety, disappointment, fear, frustration, longing: just like Bethany struggling through a conversation with an old friend in the produce section, we treat these thoughts and feelings that come up inside us as if they could tear us limb from limb if we let them.

Think over the past hour or so again. Look at the behaviors you wrote down. How much of what you did was to get you away from something coming up inside? Maybe you didn't even think much about it. You hurt, so you did something to not hurt. Think over the past day. How much of what you did was about running just ahead of a nagging worry? Or shoving some memory or fear back down out of your immediate sight? Or convincing yourself that some thought creeping up isn't true, that some feeling that keeps coming up isn't valid? How much time did you spend trying to get rid of some bit of your world in that moment?

In the psychological flexibility model, we call this *experiential avoidance,* and we think it's at the root of most human struggles. People are constantly trying to manage their experiences. Even avoiding situations, activities, people, or events in the world is about avoiding the thoughts and feelings related to those situations. You might decline a call because just seeing the name on your phone makes you annoyed. You might apologize to someone because just seeing the person makes you feel guilty. You might have a drink because thinking about the next day makes you feel stressed. You might skip a meeting or class because being there makes you feel stupid. You might make a contingency plan because thinking about the unknown makes you scared. You might spend hours dressing or grooming because imagining being around people makes you feel disgusting.

Your Avoidance

Each of us carries with us a unique set of past experiences, which means that each of us experiences the world differently. Something you'd work for may be something another person would work hard to get away from. And not only that: avoidance itself looks a little different for each of us. Finally, as self-aware as humans are, we are not always great at knowing why, how, and when it is we do the things we do. It's worth taking a moment now to notice the kinds of experiences you avoid and what that avoidance looks like for you. If you're following along on the audio files that came with this book, please play track 10 at this time.

PRACTICE: Noticing Your Avoidance

Take a slow breath and, as you exhale, let your eyes fall closed. And breathe.

And as you breathe, take a moment to notice the experience of breathing—what it feels like to pull air into your body and to release. And breathe. And let it be that with each breath, you settle more and more into your skin, into your body right now. And breathe.

On your next breath, imagine that you could call to mind all of your experiences from the past week and watch them from the outside. Like a trailer for a movie about your life recently, let it be that your mind could bounce from one memory to the next, catching glimpses of different places you've been, conversations you've had, things you've done. And breathe.

When you find your awareness stuck on a particular memory, or when one memory starts to take over, see if you can't take a nice, slow breath, breathing yourself back into your body in this moment and making more and more room for all of your memories and your thoughts about those memories to gather. And breathe.

And see if you can't let your awareness touch on each memory just a little more gently, as if you were picking up something precious but fragile in order to examine it. And breathe.

From the jumble of memories, let memories of difficult moments rise up. Maybe the world was shifting in a way you were not okay with, in a way that pushed into your thoughts and feelings. Or maybe hard experiences just started coming up inside you without the world shifting much at all. And breathe.

Notice all the different things you do when your experiences are painful, uncomfortable, or frustrating. What you look like when there's hard stuff in your world. And breathe.

Let your mind settle on a single memory in which you responded to that hard experience by trying to get away from it. Watch yourself in the moment that the world shifted, and the hard thing first arose within you. Notice the tiny little changes that show up on your face, in your eyes. Recognize what it looks like from the outside when you are carrying something hard. And breathe.

And notice if you don't feel a little seed of that hurt happening for you now, in this moment. And breathe.

Let it be that time slows way down. Watch the moment when you started to work to get away from that experience seem to stretch out. Watch your behavior shift. Notice what it looks like from the outside when you are running. Or trapping. Or killing. Notice how you respond when the thing that's hurting keeps happening.

Watch the relief come, the pain fade. And breathe.

And on your next breath, let that scene fade and let rise up another instance in which you tried another way to get away from something difficult that was happening inside you. If you find yourself settling on all similar situations, or scrambling around in your thoughts trying to find the right memory to work with, take a deep breath and see if you can't let that job go. And breathe, allowing whatever hard moment shows up to just be there.

When you notice your awareness getting scattered or stuck, take a slow breath, feeling your breath pull you back into your body. And when you notice a memory starting to take over your experience, see if you can't breathe some space in between you and that memory, so that you can experience it more fully. And breathe.

Watch your moment of running or trapping or killing unfold slowly from the moment the hard experience started to bubble up inside you to the moment you found relief. Watch your face change, the way you hold your body. See if you can't recognize the instant when you started to work to get away, and the instant when relief came. And breathe.

And on your next breath let that memory fade, as another starts to rise up. If you're willing, let it be that this hard experience is one that touches something really precious to you. Again, slow the memory way down, simply noticing the moment you let go of living and started running, trapping, or killing, and the moment that experience had gone. And breathe.

And whenever you're ready, take a moment to breathe yourself back into your skin in this moment. And whenever you're ready, open your eyes.

Take a moment to jot down a bit about your experience in the practice. Draw two lines down the piece of paper you're working on, dividing it into three sections. All the way on the left, write down what happened in one of the memories you touched on, right before you started working to get away. What was going on? And then in the second column, write down how your thoughts and feelings responded ("I thought _____ and felt _____.") And in the last column, write down what you did to get away from those thoughts or feelings. Go through each of the memories that came up in the practice, then jot down a few new examples.

Take a moment now to look over the actions you wrote down. What kinds of things do you do when things get rough inside? How do you get away? Think about the different ways we humans avoid things, and notice examples of each in your own life. What does it look like when you're running? Are there certain things you do to get busy, certain ways you stay just ahead of whatever is bothering you? How do you trap stuff away? Are there things you do to put hard memories where they can't get to you? What does it look like when you're fighting and killing? Are there certain things you do to control your world, and to attack the things that hurt? What's your most common strategy for avoidance?

Now take a moment to read over the situations you wrote down. What kinds of situations are toughest for you? Is there anything you see coming up more than once? A thread that ties through each of these?

There's one thing that was part of every situation you wrote down. Whether it was central to your struggle or not, your body was part of your experience. In fact, one of the most difficult things about struggles with body image is that your body is always there to struggle with.

Avoidance and Struggles with Body Image

For many of us, something hard doesn't have to happen around us for us to have something we want to get away from. Everywhere we go, we carry with us a signal for hurt, for frustration, for disgust, for hate. If you're someone who struggles with body image, the situation that causes you pain is often the very body you inhabit. And the experiences you spend your time running from and trapping and killing are often thoughts and feelings about your body. The problem is, of course, that there's just no escaping your body.

Even so, we try and try to get away, as if one day our efforts will be rewarded. Just like any other kind of avoidance, body image avoidance can look all kinds of different ways. Some of us do what we do with other kinds of hurt—we try to squash it down or convince ourselves to feel differently. Many of us have our own set of strategies tailored especially to our struggles with body image.

Maybe you just try not to experience your body much. You try not to see your body. You get ready in the morning without a glance in the mirror and you wash without really feeling it. You avoid care and grooming that requires much attention. Anything that requires care feels like another betrayal from your body. You focus on that which restricts your body, that which reins in its impact, that which keeps you from having to remember you have a body at all.

Maybe you hide your body from others, as if, if others don't see it, it doesn't have to be real. Maybe you simply wear clothes that obscure your flaws. You might have a formula for what you wear most days. You might stay away from swimsuits, or eveningwear, or whole categories of clothing—anything sleeveless, perhaps. Maybe the small things, such as setting aside a little extra time to put on makeup or fix your hair, have grown into rituals that don't bring relief unless done just right. People don't see you unless you've prepared yourself just so. Maybe you find yourself checking, over and over, to make sure everything is still in place, hidden away. Maybe there are places you don't go and things you don't do because they would involve attention to your body. You drop out of the wedding before you have to get sized. The doctor doesn't see you much, even when she should. You don't express affection physically. You walk away from relationships when folks get close enough to want to touch you. Maybe you avoid people altogether. You're mean or absent or forgettable. You walk away from relationships before they begin.

Maybe you make efforts to change your body for good. It's become a lifestyle. You've tried every diet and spend time looking for more. You're at the gym as much as folks who work there. Maybe you've spent money you can't afford on products that promise to change the way you look. You have to have this gadget and that brush and this cream and that vitamin. You can barely watch TV or go to the store without investing in the latest thing that's going to finally end this struggle. Maybe you've tried more invasive solutions: an injection, a lift, a tuck, an augmentation.

Maybe the things you do to get away from your experience of your body aren't obviously or logically connected to your body at all. Maybe you work too hard or too long trying to feel good enough.

Maybe you drink or use drugs to bring you some peace from your body. Maybe you clean or organize or decorate because it's easier to change the way the space around you looks than the way you look. Maybe you share your body in ways you wouldn't choose because you want it to be good for something, for someone.

It's worth taking a moment to notice the things you do to get away from the way your body makes you feel. Jot down any examples that stand out for you now, just from reading the paragraphs above. Then, if you're willing, take a few moments to notice the ways you've learned to avoid your own experience of your body. If you're following along with audio files, play track 11 now.

PRACTICE: Your Body Avoidance

Take a full, deep breath and, as you exhale, let your eyes fall gently closed. Draw a few breaths, feeling yourself settle more and more into your body with each breath. And breathe.

And when you find your awareness getting scattered or stuck, give yourself a full, deep breath and let that breath call you back to your body.

And with each breath, see if you can't feel more and more room in your awareness, more and more space for your thoughts to flow through you. And breathe.

And when you feel certain thoughts or feelings taking over, see if you can't simply notice what's coming up, and breathe back in the space you need to experience fully and with clarity. And breathe.

On your next breath, let your awareness slip from your body and into your imagination. Find yourself in a safe place you know well, maybe a room from your childhood. Take a few moments now to let the details of the room fill in—notice the color of the paint on the walls, the lines of the furniture. If there are things you can't remember, make them up. As the room becomes more and more real, notice the feelings that come up here. And breathe.

And let it be that in this room you know well, you come across a large, thick book. And that even though it's not a book you recognize exactly, something about it feels familiar. Feel yourself taking the book into your arms and settling down somewhere to have a look. And breathe.

Open the book. And let it be that the book is filled with pictures, each of them from a moment of your life. Let some of the pictures be ones you recognize, ones you've seen before. Let there be others that you've never seen, ones that don't exist. Maybe even some pictures in this book show moments that couldn't have been captured on film. Notice what shows up as you recognize your life catalogued in front of you. And breathe.

Turn back to the first page of the book, and begin to work your way forward. As you turn the pages slowly, let yourself notice images from the time in your life before you began hating your body. Maybe you were very young. See how free you look in the pictures, with no need to struggle. Watch how easily you move about your world. And breathe.

Keep turning the pages, watching your body grow and change in the images as your life unfolds in front of you. And on the next page, let yourself come to a picture from the time when you first started feeling like something was wrong with the way you look. Notice how you can tell in the picture—where your discomfort shows up in your eyes or the way you hold yourself. Notice the unease that maybe nobody else can see. And breathe.

Turn a few more pages now, noticing your appearance changing in the images before you. And as your body grows, see if you can't see your discomfort in your skin grow with it. Watch as you start to develop ways to cope—your first efforts to run from or trap or kill your young body. Watch as some of the ways of protecting yourself become more and more a part of how you are. And breathe.

And on your next breath, find yourself looking at a picture of yourself, maybe just a short time ago, settled by now into the same *ways you struggle with your body today. See if you can't recall, as you look at the image before you, how those efforts began taking up more and more time and energy in your life. If you find yourself wanting to look away, let it be that staying with your image in this tough moment could bring you strength. And breathe.*

Let the next few pages show images from your life in just the past year. Notice if, by now, your struggle with your body isn't painfully familiar—the same hurts coming up, and you responding in the same ways. And breathe.

And on the last page, find yourself looking at a picture of yourself working with this book. Recall moments when you've skipped an exercise or set this book aside because we were asking something hard of you. And breathe.

And in your mind's eye, close the book and breathe your awareness back into your body right now, letting the scene and the book fade from you. And whenever you're ready, let your eyes come open.

Jot down a few more notes with things you noticed in the exercise. See if you can't put together a list of things you do to avoid your body image. Read over your list when you have it complete. What strikes you about this list? What kinds of avoidance are most common for you? Are there certain kinds of situations in which urges to avoid show up more than others? Are there things on your list that you never quite thought of like this?

If you're like most people, it might have been tough to get started recognizing avoidance in your own life. You may have other reasons you can name for why you do almost everything you wrote down. We humans just aren't very good at explaining our own behavior. This is, in part, because most of the things you wrote down probably started out with multiple causes. You do this or that to get away but also because you get access to something lovely. Once avoidance is part of the picture, though, there's not much room for anything else. Even when there are lots of other things going on besides just the hard stuff, we tend to miss it all.

Another thing you might notice is that sometimes we engage in body image avoidance even when the hard stuff coming up doesn't have anything to do with appearance. Just as Bethany's discomfort with an old friend became a sense that she was ugly and unkempt, you start to see all of the hard stuff in your life in terms of your body. You fail a math test and you find yourself skipping lunch because suddenly you feel "fat." Someone you work with embarrasses you over a mistake you made and you find yourself checking and fixing instead of trying to correct the error. Your car breaks down and you have to fight off the urge to avoid the mechanic so no one can see how disgusting you are. If you spend enough time avoiding your body, it seems that it becomes just part of what you do when things are hard. It's the easier thing, the thing you know, the thing with the more predictable outcome than facing whatever the difficulty is more directly. Easy as it is, however, body image avoidance is associated with some significant costs.

When Avoidance Doesn't Work

We humans are fabulous at running, trapping, and killing. We avoid hundreds of times a day without even thinking much about it. In fact, we do it so well that sometimes we don't notice when it doesn't work. Consider what happens when what we are running from, trapping, or killing is something that comes from our own heads. Some bit of hurt we carry with us throughout our lives—the way we hurt when things are hard. Maybe you get more anxious than most people. Maybe you find yourself scared of everything when one thing goes wrong. Maybe you carry a heavy sadness. Maybe you feel ashamed, even about things that are not your fault. Maybe you always feel alone. Consider what happens when you start trying to run from, trap, or kill that.

In most situations, it works out really well—in the short term. We generally get some initial relief from whatever we are struggling with. The memory gets shoved back down where it belongs. We keep the fear at bay. We beat the mind into submission so we can get a moment's peace. And we can breathe freely again.

For a while.

But then what? What happens right after you feel that relief? For most of us, it's not long before that experience is back. The hurt creeps back up until it's right where it was before. Or worse. Maybe it's got a new twist to it, a new connection or a new flavor. But sure enough: there it is, a new version of the hurt we carry. And often, the harder we've worked at getting away from it, the more over-whelming it is when it shows up the next time.

So we try again. After all, it worked the last time. We got a little bit of peace. And even a little bit seems pretty good when we're in the middle of our old familiar hurt. Sometimes we use the same old strategies, but sometimes we try a new way to run from, trap, or kill an experience that hurts. And every new thing we throw at hurt, at sadness, at frustration, at fear, at painful memories—every new way of avoidance we learn—is taking time and energy and resources that we could be using for other things.

What if all that time and energy we are spending trying to manage our experience just moves us away from the lives we actu-ally want to be living? Consider this: While you are searching for a way to get rid of sadness or anxiety or shame once and for all, where are the things that really matter to you? What efforts are you putting in there? And what if avoidance is not only *not* getting you closer to the life you want, but actually moving you *away* with every step?

See, the worst thing about experiential avoidance is not just that it is ineffective. The truly terrible thing about experiential avoidance is that oftentimes the things that we care most about are tucked right inside of the most painful things we know. So when we do things to get away from pain, we can't help but turn away from the things that are precious to us.

In the next practice, if you're willing, you will spend a few minutes considering the costs of your avoidance. If you're following along with the audio files, select track 12.

PRACTICE: Noticing Opportunities

Take a moment to look over the body image avoidance list you wrote down after the last practice. Starting with the first line, take some time to slowly read the first of the actions you wrote about, closing your eyes for a moment to call to mind the situations in which you've avoided your experience of your body in this way. See if you can't settle on a single memory of one of the last times you found yourself doing this. See every detail—where you were, who was there, what you were doing beforehand. Notice the thoughts and feelings you are managing within. What hurt bubbles up inside? What makes you long for relief?

As you watch the memories unfold, let yourself wonder: If those thoughts and feelings that get in your way were to suddenly lift without the situation having to change, what actions would you take here instead? What would you want to do next if you didn't have to avoid? Who would you want to be in this situation? Watch yourself being freed from the need for avoidance. What do you do instead? And breathe.

Before moving on to another memory, let your eyes come gently open and jot down just a few words as to the actions you'd like to be taking in this situation.

And on your next breath, choose another avoidant action from your list and let your eyes fall closed once more. Again, recall a specific time in which you sought relief in this way. Let the details of your memory fill in, noticing where you were, who was there, what you were doing. See if you can't see the hurt you were feeling. And breathe.

And on your next breath, let yourself wonder what it would be like if, without the situation having to change at all, your painful thoughts and feelings were to suddenly pass from you. What would you do if you didn't have to use avoidance anymore? Who would you want to be in this situation?

110

Before moving on to another memory, let your eyes come gently open and jot down just a few words as to the actions you'd like to be taking in this situation.

Give yourself some time to call to mind a few more examples of your avoidance, each time asking yourself what you would want to be doing if you weren't so busy avoiding, and jotting down just a word or two. When you've worked through three or four examples, give yourself a few deep breaths and let your eyes come open.

Take a moment now to read over the notes you jotted down. If you're like most people, your avoidance tactics are much different from the things you'd actually like to be doing. What if every situation that brings hurt also brings opportunity? Take a moment now to notice the opportunities you've missed because of avoidance and the cost it's had in your life. Take a deep breath and ask yourself: Is it okay with me to give up the things I really care about for a little bit of relief? Is that good enough? If the answer is no—if you want more from your life than bouncing from one source of relief to the next—then it may be time to try something a little different.

An Alternative: Accepting the Unacceptable

We were all born with a great capacity to get away from things that feel bad to us. This is part of what has allowed human beings to thrive in the way we have as a species. What we don't have a lot of practice with, though, is anything else. Avoidance feels automatic. Hard or scary stuff comes up and we start avoiding. We don't even think much about it. It also feels like something we have to do. In the same way most of us wouldn't open our arms to an angry cougar or a venomous snake, experiential avoidance seems like a survival issue.

Take a moment and notice how this shows up for you. If you didn't run or trap or kill when your scariest stuff showed up, what would happen?

For most of us, the answer is something like, "It'd get to me," "I'd hurt really bad," "I would be so overwhelmed, I wouldn't be able to function," or "The pain would just totally take over." It's sort of like we think *If I am trying this hard to get away from my hurt and it keeps showing up and it keeps screwing things up, how bad would it be if I weren't trying at all?* So even as the costs accrue, even as we pass up more and more opportunities, we continue avoiding, assuming that the cost of not avoiding would be even greater. But what if the costs are not because of the hurt, but because of what we do with the hurt?

What if we can only be overwhelmed by something that we are trying to defend against? Imagine that you suddenly realized that something terrifying was coming toward you at full speed. Your instinct would be to either run or trap or kill. So maybe you'd run. Of course, eventually you couldn't run anymore and it would catch up with you, panting and far from the life you were trying to live. Or maybe you'd trap it somehow, leaving it snarling behind a wall. Of course, once that wall was up, nothing else could get through, even you. And if you keep building walls in your life, there are only so many places you can go. So maybe you'd fight, and try to kill off the terror. Of course, while you were doing that, you couldn't do anything else. And the terrifying thing coming toward you is always something you bore and trained and raised up until it could match any move you have with its own. Committing to fight means fighting forever.

What if you didn't do any of those? What if you were moving through your life, and you realized something was coming toward you at full speed, and you turned and faced the terror, not with your legs flexed or your fists up or a trap ready, but with your arms open? And if you closed your arms around it and held it close for a moment, we wouldn't say you were overwhelmed by it. We'd say you embraced it. What if your job when something painful or scary or frustrating comes up is to open up enough that you can both receive it and let it pass from you?

In the psychological flexibility model, this is called *experiential acceptance*, and it involves receiving your experiences, be they painful, pleasurable, or peaceful, with full contact. It involves letting go of all of our efforts to avoid or reduce or delay or change our experiences and simply having them as they are. It means trusting yourself to be strong enough that you can be touched by something painful without it taking over.

Now, because "acceptance" is a fairly common word, you've heard all kinds of different meanings of it that don't quite fit with the flexibility model. Folks sometimes say "accept it" to mean setting your jaw, bracing yourself, and bearing something hard. From a flexibility perspective, acceptance is much different from tolerating. It doesn't mean doing your best to hold fast and pretend the hard thing isn't there. Sometimes, when someone tells you that you should "just accept it," that person is saying that you should give up on things ever being different. From a flexibility perspective, acceptance is not about whether or not something can change. The assumption is that everything does change, that everything is constantly changing. And that when it comes to our behavior, accepting the world as it is in this moment can help us choose how to change.

Finally, acceptance also isn't something you do once. From a flexibility perspective, we're not talking about "accepting the fact that…" It's not like something hard happens to you, you don't accept it for a while, then you do and the job is all done. *Experiential* acceptance is about accepting experiences, as they come up. Just because you opened up to something hard once doesn't mean you won't have to open up again and again and again, each time you notice yourself running, trapping, or killing. From a flexibility perspective, acceptance involves noticing when you're running from your own experience, noticing when you're struggling to trap some piece of it away, noticing when you're pounding away at the things coming up in your own skin. Noticing the effort you're putting into avoidance and letting all that effort go.

Acceptance is simple. It's more not doing than doing. But that doesn't mean that it's easy. In fact, acceptance is hard—really hard. It's hard because we developed avoidance as a way to stay alive. It's hard because we don't have any practice doing anything different. It's hard because the second we let go of avoidance, we feel all the things we've been trying to get away from. And most of us don't really know what it's like to feel stuff all the way. Often we don't even let ourselves feel the feelings we long for all the way. Most of us haven't really let go and fully felt joy or love or exhilaration but maybe a handful of times. What if we live in a way that's a little too distant, a little too cautious, a little too safe?

What would it be like to open yourself up to some of the stuff you've spent a long time avoiding? What would it be like to practice *body image acceptance*—to open up to your experience of your body regardless of how it feels that day? To be honest, if you've been working through this book, doing all the practices, making notes and reading them, you've already begun. Every time you even read about something difficult, it calls up something hard in your own experience. And if you keep reading, if you let yourself remember, that's a little piece of acceptance. Every time you read our invitation to write and instead of skipping to the next section, you write hard stuff down, that's acceptance. Every time you pick this book up again, knowing it's going to be uncomfortable at best, and sometimes painful, that's acceptance.

Now let's see if you can't build this practice out a little. Next, you'll practice acceptance of the difficult experiences that come up around your body. Before you begin, call to mind the last practice you did in the previous chapter, in which you saw yourself and your fused body thoughts in the mirror. If you can, turn back to the notes where you drew what you saw in the mirror. Take a moment or two to call to mind the difficult experiences that come when you face your reflection. If you're following along with the audio files, play track 13 at this time.

PRACTICE: Taking It All In (Acceptance)

Begin by taking a slow, deep breath, and release, drawing in another just when you feel your lungs empty. Feel your eyelids become heavy as you breathe in, and let them sink slowly down as you breathe out. And breathe.

And take a moment to feel yourself sinking more and more into your skin with each breath, as if your breath was creating more and more room for you to easily be in your skin with all the thoughts and feelings rushing around in your awareness. And breathe.

And on your next breath, let it be that you find yourself suddenly before a mirror. Breathe and see if you recognize the tension that comes with seeing your own body. Breathe yourself into your body, feeling what it feels like inside your skin right now. Watch your chest rise and fall in the mirror as you feel the air pass in and out. Find your eyes in the mirror. And take a moment to see yourself. Notice yourself and breathe.

And on your next breath, slowly bring your eyes to your body. Take a few moments to notice your shape in the mirror. Let your eyes trace the lines around all of your edges. Take your time as if you needed to remember every detail of every line, angle, and curve. Work your way around your body: first facing forward, then turned to one side, then with your body facing opposite the mirror. And breathe.

And as you breathe, notice the flurry of activity that's happening in your mind as you watch yourself settle into your skin in the mirror. Notice the moments when you get scattered or stuck, and breathe yourself back into your body. See if you can't, with each breath, make a little more room for all those thoughts to be there, bouncing about behind your eyes. And breathe.

And, in the space your breath is creating, see if you can notice the judgments your mind makes about your body. Let your eyes rest on each of the parts of your body most troublesome to you, one at a time. And as your eyes come to rest on that part of your body, hear what it is that your mind says is wrong with it. And breathe.

And if you find yourself wanting to turn away from your reflection or end the exercise, let it be that sticking with yourself in this moment could offer you some strength when all this comes up out in the world. And breathe.

On your next breath, realize that, once more, the judgments that come up about your body in your mind are gradually becoming visible in the mirror, just in front of that part of you. Watch as your thoughts become visible, some familiar thoughts you noticed last time, others new, still others thoughts you've not been bold enough to see in this way. And breathe.

And, as you breathe, notice that your reflection becomes more and more hidden behind your body thoughts. And breathe.

And give yourself a long, slow breath and let it be that you could reach out into the mirror and pull just one of those body thoughts from it, out of the mirror and into the space around you. Imagine you could hold it in your hand. Maybe it has a temperature, a texture. Maybe a weight. Take a few breaths to see it, feel it there, in your hand. Consider it, like you might an interesting stone or other object.

Breathe. And as you breathe, let your breath pull that thought into you. Feel it dissolve and let it be that it seeps easily into your body, as if you had space set aside for it to just be, all mixed in with everything else you carry, right there inside of you. And breathe, returning your eyes to the mirror.

Pull another judgment you have about your body from the mirror, again taking the time to feel and see it there in your hand. And breathe. And then close your hand around it and breathe it back into your body.

And continue like this, pulling body thoughts from the mirror, one by one, taking time to notice them, then closing your hand around them, and gently breathing them into your skin. And breathe.

And once you've pulled four or five of your body thoughts from the mirror, take a moment to see yourself there, uncovered. And breathe.

On your next breath, let yourself turn away from the mirror and begin moving down a corridor that opens up to your left. Let it be that when you reach the end of this corridor, you're going to face a hard but important situation that's been lurking in your life. Notice what comes up for you as you move toward the door, and when something comes up that tries to take over your experience, gently take a deep breath, close your hand around the doorknob, breathe that hard thought in, and feel your world return.

And whenever you're ready, let your eyes come open.

Take a moment now to reflect on your experience. What was it like to draw your body judgments into yourself, to make space where they could move through you? How was this different from avoidance? Are there places in your life where being able to hold your painful thoughts and feelings close, but gently, would be useful?

Just like with the exercise, you might consider practicing in front of a mirror, noticing your thoughts and feelings about your body and yourself as they come up, and imagining breathing them into your body. In this next section, you'll set goals for practicing acceptance out in the world.

Challenge and Commitment: Old Familiar

While some of the avoidance you exhibit happens in your own home while you're all alone, or in your own mind as you shove some thoughts away, much of the avoidance that really affects your life

117

happens out in the thick of things with people you love, during activities you care about, when you're trying to take care of basic things you need to do to be well and live your life with intention. For those important corners of your life to be affected, you have to take the opportunity to notice where those scary but important corners lie and practice acceptance there.

Noticing Challenging Contexts for Body Image Acceptance

Take a look back over the work that you did in this chapter. Some of the activities you did were harder for you than others. You cruised through some feeling like this is stuff you already know or think about all the time. In others you found yourself stopping and starting, falling and getting back on track, struggling the whole way through. You'll also notice that in the course of a single activity, you could be trucking along fine and suddenly get to something that completely stops you in your tracks, maybe even knocks the wind out of you.

We've all had a long, long time to suffer with some of the hurts that we carry. It's likely that the seeds of some of your hurts started when you were very young. In the next practice, you'll take a few moments to notice where these seeds were sowed and where in your life they've grown over. If you're following along with the audio files, please advance to track 14.

PRACTICE: At First Sight

Take a nice, slow breath, feeling yourself settle into your body as you recognize and greet the familiar sensations of your breathing. As you settle into your body, take a moment to notice the thoughts and feelings passing through you. Let it be that with each breath, there is more and more room for those experiences to gather and flow through you as they will. And breathe.

And on your next breath, reach back... back... back into your memory and see if you can't call to mind when you first had the sense that there was something wrong with the way you look. Maybe a sudden something happened that caused you to stop and see yourself, your body, with judgment. Maybe it was more gradual. Maybe you started with a vague feeling that something was wrong, and this discomfort shifted slowly into the sense that something was wrong with you, which eventually settled into the unavoidable sense that something was indeed wrong with your body. And breathe.

And on your next breath, notice how those tiny seeds, that sense of something being wrong, grew into hatred. Maybe slowly at first, that discomfort growing into pain, growing with your avoidance until your behavior toward your body became clearly hostile. And breathe.

Take a moment to breathe that pain, the pain of a younger you, in and out. And see if you can't continue, with each breath, to make more and more space for that pain, and all the mental stuff that came to be, without pushing you around. And breathe.

And on your next breath, call to mind the areas of your life today that bring you back there. Maybe not in terms of a specific memory, but the things that cause you to feel small again, small and vulnerable and in pain. Notice where that old familiar pain, and the old familiar struggle with that pain, comes up in your life today. And breathe.

And whenever you're ready, let your eyes come open.

Take a moment to jot down what old, familiar pain you've been carrying around with you, along with the places it shows up. These are likely the areas of your life where avoidance gets you the most stuck. You would think that we humans would pick situations that would save us from this old, scary pain, but somehow most of us keep finding ourselves in the same old struggles.

Take a moment and wonder what it would be like to finally set that struggle down. Wonder what it would be like to be able to move freely into those hardest moments and simply trust yourself to be big enough and strong enough now to have space for that pain.

Valued Commitment: Body Image Acceptance Out in Your World

And now, it's time to look over the work you did in this chapter and make three small commitments to practicing body image acceptance out in your life. Just as you did in the last couple of chapters, you should make each commitment a little more challenging and a little more meaningful to you than the one before. For each of these commitments, you'll look for body experiences you try to avoid and situations that are likely to bring those experiences up during the next week.

Start by calling to mind everything you're expecting to encounter over the next week. What kinds of plans do you have? Where will you go? Who are you likely to see and be with? What kinds of thing will you be doing? Of the different places you'll go and things you'll run into, where might body avoidance steer you in the next seven days? What body experiences are likely to come up that you just don't let yourself have? But not just that—where will your values show up, if you let them? What opportunities will you have in the next seven days or so to do something you care about? Now number a fresh page 1 through 3 with a few blank lines after each number, and begin looking over your work from this chapter.

For your first commitment, flip through your notes and look for body experiences that come up (or try to come up) just about every day, and that you avoid (or try to avoid) just about every day. Maybe you zone out when your partner shows you physical affection because it makes you too aware of your body. Maybe you change clothes four or five times while getting ready, looking for relief from the dissatisfaction you feel when you look in the mirror. Maybe you skip the gym if it's past a certain time because of who might be there to see you. This should be a small, everyday bit of avoidance that moves you away from your values.

Think about a small commitment you might make to accept some hard body experience likely to come up in the next couple of days. You'll want to be specific about the situation in which you'll practice acceptance, what thoughts and feelings you'll be accepting, and what you'll do to accept. The more specific you are with your commitment, the better. You'll start with the situation ("When I…"), then the thought or feeling ("and I think/feel…"), then exactly what you'll do ("I'll practice acceptance by…").

Challenge yourself to come up with an acceptance technique (or techniques) that works for you. Anything that involves embracing the experience instead of running from it, trapping it inside, or trying to kill it off is acceptance. It could involve simply breathing it into your body, like you did in the last exercise, making more and more room to be. You could imagine carrying it close to you, like you might carry a fussy child, even as it hurt you to be with him or her. You might assign yourself a particular thing you could do to extend the experience instead of end it. Be creative. When you're ready, write down your first commitment (in the format described above) next to the number 1.

For your second commitment, see if you can't look for a situation that's a little more challenging for you, a situation that brings up a body experience that you work a little harder to avoid. This should be something that comes up every few days or so and rocks your world a bit when it does, pushing you away from the life you want. Maybe there's a memory you carry that comes up out of nowhere every few days and tugs at the back of your mind. Maybe, like Bethany at the store, you see somebody at work or school who makes you feel particularly terrible about your appearance. Again, be specific about the situation, the experience that comes up, and what you'll do to accept it.

For your final commitment, you'll focus on an experience that you are pretty good at avoiding, something that you work hard to keep at bay. Or maybe something that you've been avoiding for so long, you don't even notice you're working at it. You might think about things you don't ever do because of the way you feel about your body. Are some of these things part of your valued life? Things that would move you toward the person you want to be? Take a moment and imagine the places you might go or actions you might take if one day that struggle with your body just fell away. Is one of those actions something you could commit to trying out this week? Take a moment and see if you can't come up with a really bold but doable commitment.

When you've got your commitments recorded, let your eyes close just briefly and notice how hard it is to commit, even just to yourself. Notice how frightening it is to reach out for something different. Once more, if you're feeling particularly bold, you might share your commitments with someone you love.

As you set off into your next week, remember to hold these commitments lightly. If something you committed to is turning out to be more difficult, you might shift the commitment to something you can reach with just a little step forward. If a situation presents itself that you hadn't thought of, feel free to change your commitments up. Mark your commitments off when you complete them. And if, at the end of this week, you still haven't stepped into an acceptance practice, give yourself a whole new round of commitments and another week. Sometimes we need more time and space to grow in ways that really matter.

6 Your Body, Your Self: Getting to Know You

Who are you? No, *really*. Imagine that someone asked you right now, walked right up to you, and said, "Hey—who are you?" Take a moment to think about it. What would be the first things to come up for you? How would you respond?

Now go ahead and think back to all the ways you've answered that question in the past. Notice how the answer shifted depending on where you were and what you were up to: "My name is Susan." "It's me, Jim!" Maybe you explained your role in that situation. "I'm a professor here." "I'm a visiting parent." "I'm the customer who called earlier." "I'm a presenter." Or maybe you described your relationship to someone else. "I'm Jonathan's wife." "I'm the bride's cousin." "I'm Hannah's mom." "I'm Anne's daughter."

And all that might be true and even meaningful to you, but is it you? Are any of those what makes you *you*?

How It Goes: We Are the World

We humans have a lot of information going in and out of our awareness all the time. Think back to the monitors. Our experience in any one moment is incredibly rich. You've got the constantly changing world that you can see and hear and taste and smell and feel. You've got the constant flow of emotions, shifting in how intense they are, how positive or negative they feel. You've got your mind's constant labels, evaluations, and comparisons making sense of everything else coming up for you. And as the moments are strung together over time, we build a history with the world. We learn about what the world has to offer and we develop ways of navigating it, all of which work really well in some ways and really terribly in others.

Something else is happening as we learn about the world—something we usually don't even notice. As the world and your experience of the world is constantly shifting and changing, there is one thing that is always present: you. Throughout every experience you've known, you've always been there. You've always been witnessing your life unfolding, even before you had any words to make sense of it. With everything you've ever noticed, you were there to do the noticing. Even as you read these words, you might notice that in addition to the words in front of you and the thoughts they bring up and the sensations in your body and the sounds around you, there's *you*—steady and constant, even as your world flows and shifts and changes.

One thing that seems to be really special about humans is that as we learn about the world, we also come to learn about ourselves. We are self-aware, and we're able to be self-aware because of how we use language to bring bits of the world along with us. From the time you were very, very small, you were asked questions that you had to pay attention to your unique experience to answer. "Are you hungry?" "Does your foot hurt?" "Do you like that?" "What do you want to do next?" "Do you see the ball?" "What are you doing?"

Pretty early on, you learned that these questions are different from ones like, "What color is this?" or "Where is Dolly?" To answer all those "you" questions, you attend to two things: some particular aspect of your experience and the self that's having the experience. You are the "I" that you speak from and the "you" that others speak to you about. You have a name that separates you from everything else in the world. Pretty soon you can generate statements about where you are, what you're doing, what you're feeling and thinking. And not only in this moment right now; you can also think back to things you experienced before and anticipate the things you might experience later and say what happened before and what will happen next. Meanwhile, while all this noticing is going on, you're learning more and more about yourself. And what do you learn? You learn to connect certain aspects of your experience to an idea of who you are.

Some of what we learn about us is based on our feelings. Soon after we are born, we start getting asked if we're sad, if we're excited, if we're mad. And soon, a whole chunk of our awareness is set aside for feelings coming up inside of us. Butterflies in your stomach are something different from a warm fuzzy feeling. The older we get, the more different kinds of feelings we recognize. The tightness in your chest can be excitement or nervousness, depending on what else is going on. But as obvious as our own feelings are to us, we can't always tell what others are feeling by observing them. Your feelings are a world all for you, and the same is true for everyone else. You come to know the familiar feelings and what they feel like when they start to come up. You know ones that you long for and ones you struggle with. Your feelings are yours. And sometimes, it seems your feelings *are* you. We don't often say we *feel* sad, we say we *are* sad. And if you *are* sad long enough, in enough different situations, it seems you're just a sad guy.

But we don't learn only from the inside out. Some of what we learn about ourselves is based on our behavior. We learn to watch ourselves. We watch what we're doing so we can report back. "Are you eating?" "Where are you going?" "Whatcha doin'?" We watch how we do things, and how that works out for us. We watch what we do so we can copy others. When we watch ourselves doing the same thing again and again, we turn that into something about us. Call to mind how young you were when you first learned to evaluate if you were a "good boy" or a "good girl." For most of us, soon after we learned there was an "us," we learned to evaluate ourselves. If you always get the right answer, you're smart. If you drop things and trip over your feet, you're clumsy. If you do things that are scary, you're brave. If you don't do things you're supposed to, you're lazy.

And it's not just about us. Some of what we learn about ourselves is how we are connected to other people. We learn early on that many of the people in our lives with special names like "mom" or "grandpa" or "sister" are important in helping us get what we need and want. It works out when we give them special attention. And not only that, we learn that who they are determines some of who we are. When mom is around, you are "son" or "daughter." Your brother or sister makes you "brother" or "sister." Connecting with someone outside of your family makes you both "friends."

And some connections are bigger than just two people. Some of what we learn about ourselves is where we belong. We learn that some folks are bound together as a family or a class or a team or a club or just a group of friends. You learned that you were part of the Smiths, and Mrs. Gordon's class, and the Rockets, and the Scouts, and the kids who play superheroes by the back trees at recess. We learn that some folks are bound together because they live in a certain place or speak a certain language or look a certain way or do certain things. You are American and Black. You are a woman and gay. You are Catholic and a New Yorker. And we learn quickly, maybe too quickly, that folks inside the group always seem a bit better and better off than those outside the group. So the part of you that is part of something bigger is something to care for, something to protect, something to keep.

And soon after we learn to pay attention to other people, we come to imagine what other people see. Some of what we learn about ourselves is what we look like from the outside. We recognize others by how they look and also learn that it's through our appearance that they recognize us. We learn that others can see the face that we see from, that our bodies look different from across the room than what we see. And we learn that appearance can be important. We notice how things work out well when we look one way and not so well when we look another. We learn to seek out our reflections so we can see whom others must see. We learn to manage how we look so we can manage who we are.

PRACTICE: Seeing "I Am"

Before we go any farther into this chapter, it's worth taking a few minutes to consider the experiences you've had that you've connected with who you are—the experiences you recognize as you. Number a page from 1 to 35 and write next to each number, "I am." Once you have a page of 35 "I am's," set a timer for three minutes. Take a deep breath, start the timer, and complete the sentences so that each reads, "I am…" Don't stop until the timer is finished or until you've completed 35 sentences.

When you've got your list of 35 sentences, let your eyes come closed for a minute and give yourself a few breaths. Then take a look at what you've written. This is the kind of exercise you could have done for 30 minutes and still had more to write. Generally, though, those first few minutes give you a good sense of how you're relating to yourself these days. What kinds of things show up for you when you think about who you are? Notice the different ways you come to know yourself: your feelings, your behaviors, your relationships, your groups, and finally, your appearance. Were all of these represented in your list? Were any categories strangely missing? What categories were best represented in your list? Did anything keep coming back up as you wrote? Were there things that came up that you decided not to write down? Were there things on your list that surprised you?

And now—of all of these 35 things that are you, are some of them more you? Do some of the things you wrote feel really true, like parts of you that you really hold on to? Do some of the things you wrote seem not to fit anymore now that you've gotten some space from the practice? Do any of the things you wrote seem to conflict with one another? Are you both happy and sad? Stupid and smart? Kind and mean?

Now take a moment to notice how your experience of yourself changes as you find yourself in different kinds of situations, with different people, doing different things. In fact, just as your experience of the world is constantly changing, your experiences of yourself vary from moment to moment.

And now, ask yourself this question: If you gave this piece of paper to someone you didn't know, and let them read these things you associate with yourself, what would be the impact? Would he or she know you? Having read all these little pieces of how you see yourself, would a stranger understand who you are and what you're about?

If not, what would be missing?

The "You" in Your Struggles with Body Image

For better or for worse, the way that we look strongly influences how others see us. As kids we learn that people's looks can tell us a lot about them. We can tell a police officer and a doctor apart based on clothing. The expression on a person's face tells us how she is feeling. What someone looks like can tell us how old he is and who he is related to. And, as influential as appearance is on the way we see the outside world, it has perhaps an even greater effect on how we feel inside.

For one, most of us learned as kids that appearing a certain way could make folks think bad things about us. We may have heard things like, "Let me brush that hair. We don't want people to think I'm not taking care of you!" We also learned that appearing a certain way could hide bad things about us. "There you go. Now no one will ever know how terrible you're feeling!" In addition, right alongside those warnings about what folks might think, and the efforts to manage that, we heard others being evaluated on the basis of their appearance. Our parent might say, "He just does not look like a very nice boy." A teacher might say with warm affection in her eyes, "What a good-lookin' kid," or, "You always look so cute. Where does your mommy get your clothes?" Finally, we come to learn, not only is appearance something that is noticed and evaluated, it's something that can determine how we are treated. We might notice that when we hear, "What beautiful blue eyes," or "You're so long and lean," or "You were the cutest one up there," we get the most attention, or the biggest smiles, or the sweetest hugs.

Eventually, it can come to seem that what you look like is who you are. You start to manage your look as a way of managing how others think and feel about you. And, perhaps more importantly, you start to manage your look as a way of managing how you feel about yourself.

Take a moment to look over your list of "I am's," noticing any that are specifically about the way that you look. You may have described your body size or your hair color—"I am too skinny" or "I am brunette." You may have written down evaluations of your appearance—"I am beautiful" or "I am hideous."

Now look at the "I am's" you wrote that are not specifically about your body. See if you don't have a pretty clear image tucked away of what you look like for most. For those of us who struggle with body image, even those parts of us that have nothing to do with how we look have everything to do with how we see ourselves.

I Am and I Do

Another way to consider your "I am's" is in terms of how they work in your life. Glance over your list again. Except this time, don't ask yourself how true the statements you wrote are. Ask yourself instead what it's like for you when each feels perfectly true or is very strongly present for you. How does that experience affect your behavior when it's really present? You might notice that not every "I am" statement you wrote influences you the same way. Some ways of experiencing yourself seem to move you closer to who you are trying to be, and others get in the way.

For example, some of the "I am's" on your list are things that seem to come from what others see in you or what others have chosen for you. Maybe you've got a piece from your past that hangs on in people's minds even though it's been over for a long time. Maybe you've got the sense that everyone thinks you have some quality that you really don't have. Maybe you've discovered something about yourself that you're pretty sure wouldn't be okay with the folks you know. Maybe the folks in your life want something for you so badly that you've been willing to bend and stretch and tuck to try to be that. Maybe you give people what they expect, even though you know you've got more inside you. Or maybe, for you, it's just the opposite—maybe you do the opposite of what people want for you or expect from you just because they want or expect it. Sometimes we take on the things people see in us and of us in the same way we might slip into a mask and costume. The problem is, of course, that this keeps us from stretching out into what we really want to be.

Take a look at your list now and underline any "I am's" you wrote down that are like this—that seem to be about meeting (or defying) others' expectations or wishes for you.

Not every experience of ourselves that holds us back comes from others. We spend lots of our time evaluating ourselves and deciding what we are that is good and what we are that is not good enough. And not only that: We make tons of rules all on our own about what we must be and what we can't ever be. Not only do these not *have* to come from others, sometimes it seems that they *couldn't*. Sometimes we have the sense that there are things about us, things that we are, that people don't know and really shouldn't, or couldn't, ever know. Sometimes these things grow until life seems to be about not getting discovered for what we really are (or are not).

Take a look at your list now and underline any "I am's" you wrote down that are like this—that seem to be about how you are not good enough or how you must be exceptional.

Some of the experiences of ourselves that hold us back are not evaluations we hold or expectations others have for us. They are relationships you have or roles you play or things you do that are certainly true and no one would say otherwise. You are a sister, you are a student, you are an ice skater. And even facts about you can disrupt your ability to live the life you care about. The problem is in the way we hold on to these labels and what they mean. Sometimes, the qualities that make us who we are seem so important, and so important to do right, that we find ourselves working harder and harder to try to fit that thing that we already are. Sometimes we work at that until other things start to suffer. Sometimes, the harder we work at being something, the more it seems to slip away.

Take a look at your list now and underline any "I am's" you wrote down that you tend to hold onto a little too tightly.

Now look at all the "I am's" you underlined on your list. Just as we get fused with different experiences of the world, we get fused even more easily with different experiences of ourselves. As our experience of ourselves shifts and changes, every once in a while an "I am" shows up that completely takes over. Fused-self thoughts limit the possibilities you see for yourself, and thereby your life. And, in doing so, they often limit your behavior. In the next practice, you'll get a sense of how fusion with different experiences of yourself works for you.

PRACTICE: You-Fusion

Start by taking a slow, full breath. See if you can feel the air coming into your body, the way your body shifts to make room for it. Hold it for just a moment before releasing. And breathe.

Now take a look at the list of "I am's" you created, noticing the thoughts and feelings that come up as you read each one. Imagine that as you breathe and read through your list, you're breathing more and more room for the "I am's" you're calling up. And breathe.

And on your next breath, take your pen or pencil and draw a line through what you wrote next to "I am" for number 4. As you cross out this thing that you see as you, imagine that that aspect of you was no more. Take a moment to notice what it feels like to let that experience of yourself go. And breathe.

And on your next breath, take your pen or pencil and draw a line through what you wrote next to "I am" for number 21. And as you cross this one out, imagine that that aspect of you was no more. Take a moment to notice what it feels like to let that experience of yourself go. And breathe.

And on your next breath, take your pen or pencil and draw a line through number 13, imagining that this thing about you were to come to an end. As you cross it out, feel yourself letting it go. Notice what that letting go feels like. And breathe.

And on your next breath, cross out 2 and 25. Notice. And breathe.

And 14 and 6. Notice. And breathe.

Cross out 17 and 22 and 11. Notice. And breathe.

And on your next breath, cross out everything you have left next to "I am" for numbers less than 6 and greater than 16, imagining opening yourself way up and letting those things go. And breathe.

Now give yourself three slow breaths as you cross out everything left that you wrote next to "I am," one by one. Let it be that each of these things that you know about you were to suddenly be no more. And breathe.

And on your next breath, notice what's left on your page. And let yourself wonder—

If everything you know about yourself were to change, if each of these things were to slip from you, would you still be you? If, over time, all you really knew about yourself was what was left on this page, would you still be a whole, complete person? Notice the first thoughts that come up for you, then see if you can't open up a little more. Continue to wonder, watching your thoughts. And breathe.

What was that like for you? If you're like most people, crossing out some of your "I am's" was a real relief, like, "Wow! That could just go away." Other things on your list were probably harder to cross out. You may have found yourself really resisting even imagining that they were no more by not crossing the words out or by arguing that that thing about you could never change. Of course, anything you wrote down could change—if not literally, then in your experience of yourself. If you are a woman, you could have a series of experiences that caused you to feel less and less like a woman, even without gender reassignment. If you are a brother or a sister, and you outlived all your siblings, you might feel that part of you slipping away.

There are many ways we come to know ourselves, such as by noticing what we do, what we think, with whom we connect, groups of which we're a part, and how we look. And each of these involves watching ourselves, then naming or evaluating what we see. Each of these involves some conceptualization of ourselves, some idea about who we are. And, for most of us, those ideas are both what we get to know and what we hope to manage and protect. For most of us, imagining letting go of those ideas is like imagining no longer existing. So even as we change and ideas about who we are no longer fit, we hold on.

But just as knowing about someone is not the same as knowing them, *knowing about* yourself, even everything about yourself, is not the same as *knowing* yourself. What if knowing yourself means knowing the you that is more than any idea about you—the you that is more than all the ideas put together? What if knowing yourself means knowing the you that would still be there if everything about you changed or went away? What if knowing yourself means knowing both the conceptualizations and the one doing the conceptualizing?

An Alternative: Knowing You, the World Apart

There is a you behind your eyes that is reading these words right now, and noticing not only what you are reading, but that it's you reading. There is a you that is there to hold feelings of shame and feelings of pride, feelings of dread and feelings of anticipation. And a you that notices what it's like to hold those feelings. There is a you that watches the constant thinking, the constant naming and comparing and evaluating, a you that watches the words form around your experiences as quickly as they come. And there's a you that notices you watching. Even as you read the words in this book, you can hear the words in your head, notice the thoughts they bring up, and also notice yourself here and now, and with your thoughts.

One way of knowing yourself involves knowing the you that is consistent, even as the worlds around you and inside you shift and change. Think back to the beginning of the chapter when we talked about how you come to know yourself. Shortly after we're born, we begin putting words on our experiences, some of which are uniquely our own. "I am hungry." "I am sad." "I like bananas." "I was singing." "I fell down." "I am going to grandma's." In doing so, we separate our immediate selves, our own perspective, from the rest of the world. *I* is different from *you*. *Here* is different from *there*. *Now* is different from *then*. Once we begin putting words like "I" or "me" on our experience, though, once we name it as a concept, we can't help but attach it to all kinds of other stuff: the way we look, the things we do, the roles we have, the ways we're good and bad. And with every little detail we add to our conceptualizations of ourselves, we get a little further from noticing the lens that we always look through, the us that is always there. With everything we come to know about ourselves, we lose touch with the part that holds it all without being defined by it.

So how do we unlearn everything we've come to know about ourselves? Well, we don't. Just like any other thoughts, we can't take away what doesn't work or isn't true. So your conceptual self—all those things you *know* about yourself—that isn't going anywhere. But taking time to notice the thoughts, and the you that's having the thoughts, can help you to *have* thoughts without *being* them. If you're following along with the audio files, please select track 15.

PRACTICE: I-Contact

Take a slow, deep breath and, on your exhale, let your eyes fall gently closed. Give yourself a few breaths as you settle more and more into your skin right now. Feel the breath flowing in and out of your body, feel your weight in the room. And breathe.

And on your next breath, imagine that there is a hand mirror in your hands, a mirror big enough that you can see your whole face in it at once. Take a moment to feel the mirror on your skin before raising the mirror so that you are holding it in front of you. And breathe.

Take a moment to recognize yourself in the mirror, your familiar face as it is here and now. And breathe.

And on your next breath, let your eyes come to rest on the top of your head. Notice the silhouette of your head, the edge between you and the rest of the world. Notice the hair or skin that covers your head—the colors you see there, the way the light touches you there. And breathe. Let your eyes move to the edge of your face and trace, with your eyes, the line where your scalp ends and your face begins. And breathe.

135

And gently shift to notice your forehead, the space between your scalp and your eyebrows. Notice the creases your laughter, your surprise, your pain have carved there. And breathe. Notice the curve of your eyebrows. The way the hair is distributed there. And breathe.

Now let your eyes trace around to your cheekbones. Notice the color there, the shape they take. And breathe.

Trace your jaw and around to your chin. Notice the shape of your lips. See if you can see where your lips begin, where the color shifts from that of your skin. And breathe.

And on your next breath, move gently up the cleft above your lips to your nose, circling your nostrils and noticing the slope of your nose, where it shifts into cheek. And breathe.

And as you breathe, notice the way your skin creases in the soft places around your eyes. Notice the way your eyelids rest on your eyes, your lashes fanning outward. And breathe.

And finally, let your awareness come to rest on your own eyes. As you gaze into your eyes, notice the swirl of colors there. Try to pick out every distinct shade you can. The flecks of brown and green and gray and gold and blue. And breathe.

And now, I'd ask you to look just beyond the shape and colors and notice in your eyes the things they have seen. As you gaze into your own eyes, see if you can't recognize there someone who has truly loved you. Notice what it's like to have known love and acceptance. And breathe.

And on your next breath, notice the thoughtfulness you show to people around you. See in your eyes the joy you get out of making someone feel loved. And breathe.

Recognize the struggle you've had with your body, the loathing you've known, the sense of loss or confusion or hopelessness that creeps up in still moments. And breathe.

And as you look into your eyes, see if you can't recognize the memories your eyes hold.

See the first person you called a friend and really, really meant it. See the first teacher you remember taking an interest in you. See the memory of them rise up in your eyes and let their names echo around you. And breathe.

And on your next breath, recognize the memory of a time you fell down and cried until someone came. And the memory of a time you fell down and pretended it didn't hurt. And breathe.

Gaze into your own eyes and see a time your face went hot with shame. And another. And another. And breathe.

Peer into your eyes and see a time that you really thought you were in love. And another. And another. And breathe.

Let yourself notice the memories that loom like shadows there in your eyes. The ones that catch your breath and turn your stomach. The ones you try your best to push away. And breathe.

Recognize in your eyes yourself as a daughter or son. And breathe. Recognize in your eyes yourself as a student. And breathe. Recognize in your eyes yourself as a friend. And breathe. As a customer. As a stranger. And breathe. And breathe.

And as you breathe, notice the whole of your experiences there, pouring from your own eyes. And breathe.

And notice that they are your eyes. Your browns and blues and greens and golds and grays, under your lids with fanning lashes, under your eyebrows, above your cheeks. Take a moment to recognize that you are there, behind those eyes, receiving what the moment has to offer, holding the memories that rise up.

And whenever you're ready, give yourself one last full breath, and let your eyes come open.

Take a moment now to ask yourself again the question we began with: *Who are you?* And notice the you that's both asking and receiving the question. Notice the answers that come up, and the you, here and now, in which those answers come up. And breathe, noticing both the experience of breathing and the you that is both breathing and experiencing.

Challenge and Commitment: Knowing You, Knowing Others

There is an intimate connection between knowing yourself and knowing others. And while we are out in the world building a concept of ourselves, we are simultaneously building concepts of others. We take what we see in another, how we feel when we are with them, the thoughts we have about them. And in sorting out who other people are, what they offer us, how they compare to us or others we know, we create a *them* that is simply our experience of them. You feel comfortable with him, so he is welcoming. You feel excited when she is around, so she is fun. You feel anxious when she talks to you, so she is pushy. And just like we collect "I am's," we can't help but do "he is" and "she is" all day.

The problem is, of course, that if you are not defined by your experiences, certainly others can't be defined by what you experience of them. Just as your conceptualization of you makes it hard to connect with yourself, to notice your own perspective, so your conceptualization of others makes it hard to connect with others, to notice their perspective. We become fused with thoughts and feelings that show up when people are around, and we miss out on really seeing them.

Take a moment and call to mind a time when you could tell you were not being seen—a time when someone clearly had an idea of who you are and what you're about, and was treating you as if it were true. When was the last time you felt really misunderstood? Maybe you've felt someone making assumptions about what you like or what you believe. Maybe you've felt someone treating you as if you weren't capable of much. Maybe you've felt someone taking more from you than you were willing to give. Maybe you've felt someone protecting him- or herself from you, as if you were dangerous. What was that like for you? Notice that the important thing is not whether what the person saw in you was correct, but the impact it had on him or her. That person missed you and probably didn't even know it. That person missed that you were more than his or her personal experience of you.

What was that like for you? Take a moment and call to mind how you responded. And now, what do you supposed it's been like for the folks you've misunderstood? How do you suppose they knew you were missing out on who they really are? Think back to how they responded. Do you have a sense of how that affected your relationships with them? How about your relationship with yourself?

The cost of fusion with our judgments of others is not just about how it hurts them or hurts our relationships with them. For most of us, it has a direct impact on how we treat ourselves. The more we act like others *are* our experiences of them, the more we do so toward ourselves. What if you can't fully acknowledge and make contact with your own perspective until you're able and willing to take the perspective of another? What if the only way to really know another fully is to acknowledge your experience of him or her, and then add to it by imagining what it must be like inside his or her skin? What if the only way to really know yourself fully is to acknowledge your experience of another, then add to it by imagining what it must be like inside his or her skin?

Next, we'll take a few moments to practice dipping in to the perspective of another and letting that move you. If you're following along with the audio files, please turn to track 16.

PRACTICE: Approaching Connection

Take a nice, deep breath, and, on the exhale, let your eyes fall gently closed. Take just a few moments to breathe, letting yourself settle more and more into your skin with each breath.

Let it be that with each breath you have more and more room for your experiences to gather where you can observe them, before they pass through you. And breathe.

And on your next breath, call to mind a safe place you've known—either from actual memory or something you've imagined before. And let it be that you suddenly find yourself there. Breathe the air in that safe place in and out, and look around you, noticing the tiny little details of the world there. And breathe.

And let it be that you are suddenly aware of another person there with you, someone you've been struggling with, someone who is difficult for you. Notice what it's like to have that person here, in your space. And see if you can't breathe that in and out, making more room for it with each breath. And breathe.

And as you breathe, let yourself notice that somehow, this person is unaware of your presence.

Take a step toward this person that you've struggled with, noticing what comes up as you move just a little closer to him or her. And breathe.

And on your next breath, move close enough now to notice how this person holds his or her body. See if you can't see the burden of this struggle in the posture. Maybe the person stiffens against it, staying hard and proud. Maybe he or she crumbles a little more each day under this weight. Let your eyes pass over this person's body from the top of the head to the feet, seeing if you can't rest your eyes in all the places you can see the struggle taking hold. And breathe.

And as you breathe in and out, take a step with each exhale until you are standing just beside this person you've struggled with, this person who is difficult for you. Let it be that, even as you get right next to him or her, the person still does not notice you. And breathe.

Let your eyes come to rest on this person's eyes and imagine that, as the person gazes out at the world, you peer into those eyes. Imagine that as you look, you recognize suddenly the way the struggle he or she has known shows up in those eyes. See if you can't see it deep behind the eyes, and recognize what it is this person must be feeling. And breathe.

And when you long to look away, see if you can't notice that longing, along with everything else that's coming up. See if you can't recognize this person's own desire to run away, right there behind the eyes. And breathe.

On your next breath, let it be that you peer a little closer to this person you've struggled to accept. And as you lean in, that suddenly signs of the struggle begin to creep to the surface. Maybe you see the eyes begin to fill with tears, maybe the forehead or brows begin to furrow. Maybe the jaw becomes increasingly set. Imagine that you could understand, more and more, the difficulties this person carries. Watch as he or she is moved by this experience. And breathe.

And as you breathe in and out, let it be that with each breath, you could open yourself up more and more to letting yourself be moved by this person you've struggled with. And breathe.

And on your next breath, let the scene begin to fade from you as you breathe your way back into your skin in this moment, right now. Take three slow, deep breaths. And breathe.

And whenever you're ready, let your eyes come open.

Before moving on to anything else, take out a piece of paper or a notebook and write yourself a letter from the person you just imagined. What might this person say to you if tomorrow he or she woke up with the courage? What might he or she want you to hear? Give yourself ten minutes or so to craft the letter.

When you're finished, give yourself a few slow breaths before reading this letter you wrote. As you read over the letter, take time to notice the similarities and differences in the way you talk to yourself and the way this person you've struggled with talks to you. What do you notice?

Valued Commitment: Knowing Folks in the World Beyond Appearances

Just like in all the preceding chapters, it's time now to read over the work you've done in this chapter and to make three small commitments to practicing knowing folks (including you) beyond what you see. Just like in the previous chapters, each commitment should be a little more challenging and a little more meaningful to you and your valued life than the one before. For each of these commitments, you'll look for body experiences that interfere with contacting your and others' perspectives in a way that moves you toward being who you want to be.

Start by calling to mind the places you'll go, things you'll do, and people you'll see over the next week. Hesitate just a moment to reflect over the opportunities you'll have to connect with your own perspective, quiet moments when you might step back and notice the you through which all your experiences flow. Now consider the opportunities you'll have to connect with the perspectives of others, moments when you might stop and imagine what it must be like to feel the way they are feeling right now, to struggle in the way they are struggling today. Notice the opportunities that, when they come up, feel connected to your values, consistent with the valued life you've been working so hard to build. Find a fresh page to work on, and write the numbers 1 through 3 with a few blank lines after every number.

For your first commitment, think about a situation in which you tend to experience yourself very narrowly. Consider situations in which you step firmly into a role (formal or not) and let that role define you. Maybe you find yourself being someone at work that you don't really recognize, losing touch with how to really talk to others or work with them. Maybe you watch yourself slipping into the stance of an angry teenager whenever you're corrected. Maybe you recognize that you mimic your mom or dad in your home life. Maybe you watch yourself sink into anxiety or depression to the point that that is the defining feature of your life. Call to mind the times when you're the nice one or the mean one or the smart one or the dumb one, and watch what it looks like from the outside as you move further and further from the you you want to be.

Now consider some small commitment you might make to stop and notice you, your self, in the moment, as the one through which all of these experiences are flowing. Be specific about where this situation occurs and what experiences come up there that limit how you see yourself and how you behave, and decide how you'll go about noticing your experiences and your self. Challenge yourself to think of a perspective-taking exercise that fits for you. You might imagine your eyes in the mirror, and see if you can't recognize what you are experiencing in your eyes. You might imagine you could see yourself from the outside. You might take a moment to envision your experiences flowing into your body and through, as you breathe in and out.

When you have chosen a commitment, take a moment to write it down next to number 1. Give yourself one or two days to get this commitment done. The more specific your commitment, the more likely it will be that you'll give it a shot. You'll want to start with the situation ("When I…"), then the thought or feeling ("and I think/ feel…"), then exactly what you'll do ("I'll practice noticing my perspective by…").

For your second commitment, see if you can't bring up a role or experience that you take on fairly often, one that tends to define you and the people you interact with. Let yourself notice experiences that cause you not only to see yourself in a certain, limited way, but also keep you seeing a certain person, group of people, or others generally in a certain way. Maybe when you're feeling beat down like some kind of victim, you treat everyone else as if they were cruel. Maybe when you are feeling down or anxious, you treat the people who love you as if they are naive to hurt and couldn't possibly understand. Maybe when you're feeling like a grumpy child, you treat others as though they are responsible for you. Again, be specific in your commitment about when this is likely to come up, what roles will start to swallow you, what roles you'll put on others, and what you'll do to see you and others more broadly as people, each with experiences flowing through us all the time. Give yourself three to five days to take this commitment on.

For your final commitment, call up an experience of yourself that you tend to hold onto pretty tightly, maybe an "I am" that was hard to cross off in the exercise. This might be something that seems really central to who you are, to what makes you different from everyone else. Call to mind interactions with others that challenge this "I am," and notice what you see in them in those moments when you've got a death grip on your experience. Think about the moments when you feel most isolated, most alone, and notice what experience separates you from all others in your mind. Approach this final commitment slowly, imagining how you might find yourself venturing through the barriers you set up to connect with the people you love. Give yourself a week or so to fulfill this commitment.

When you've got your commitments recorded, let your eyes close just briefly and notice what it's like to commit. Notice how scary it is to question the way you've always done things, and to dare to hope that you could do more. As always, if you're feeling particularly bold, you might share your commitments with someone you love.

And now, before you start the clock on your commitments, see if you can't offer them to yourself as gifts rather than burdens, choices rather than have-to's. And if, over the course of the week, you find yourself treating yourself like a victim of your own choices, set your commitments down for a moment, and don't pick them up until you can do so as a free choice.

1 You Get to Pick: Choosing Direction

A while back, you picked up a book you weren't quite sure about and started reading. Maybe you knew what you were looking for. Maybe you were looking for a way out or an ultimate solution. Maybe you didn't dare look for anything. Maybe someone gave you this book and you felt like you had to give it a try. Maybe your curiosity finally got the best of you. Either way, we're going to guess that what you found—our talk about pain and freedom—was probably not exactly what you expected. And yet, something kept you reading. Something kept you trying out our invitations, even when it really hurt, even when you had no idea why. Something kept you coming back.

In chapter 2, we started asking you to think about the life you would have if your struggle with your body image couldn't keep you from really living anymore. And, if you were bold, you let yourself wonder. You let yourself imagine. You let yourself perhaps not believe, but hope, that everything could be different for you, without your body, or your hatred for your body, having to change. And your hard work didn't stop there. When you were willing, you noticed things about yourself, your thoughts and feelings, and your world that you've never noticed before. When you were committed, you took steps in your life that moved you toward being the person you want to be.

And now, as we reach the end of our journey together, the challenge is for you to not only continue what you've started—to keep noticing opportunities and obstacles, to keep choosing and committing to new things—but also to take over our job of continuously inviting you back to your valued life. Now, we're going to go ahead and guess that this won't be easy. Like most of us, you've spent a long time treating yourself like something shameful that must be fixed, or hidden, or beaten into shape. And, for our last invitations, we're going to invite you to do something different.

PRACTICE: Between the Rules

Take a moment to draw a nice, full breath, letting your eyes sink closed on your exhale. And breathe.

Now call to mind your day yesterday, starting with the moment you woke up. Notice where you were when you first became aware of yourself and your world. When you pulled your eyes open. See how you first pulled yourself from where you sleep, and watch yourself move into the first thing you do when you wake up. And breathe.

And on your next breath, leave those first moments and move out into the rest of your day. Watch yourself move about your world, the places you take yourself, the things you do, the people you connect (or don't connect) with. And breathe.

And as you watch yourself and your world interact, see if you can't pick out things you wish you'd handled differently. These situations don't have to be big situations with serious consequences. They can be little things that you would just like to do differently. In the moments when you get stuck and can't think of anything, shift your attention to be aware of the consequences of the things

146

you do. If you don't like the consequence, perhaps there's something you'd want to do differently. When you land solidly on a memory of something you'd like to do differently, open your eyes and jot down a few notes of what you'd like to do differently, then return to the practice.

Let it be that each time you return to this practice, you return a little more fully, with a little less defensiveness against what you might see there. And breathe.

And when you have four or five things jotted down, give yourself one last breath, and let your eyes come open.

Now, take a moment to look over the things you've written down. What's it like to read over these things you'd like to change about how you're living? Imagine you had a week to get your life the way you want it. What would it be like to take a week or so and try to address these? Notice what comes up for you as you imagine simply choosing to do things a little differently.

How It Goes: Shoulds, Have-To's, Can'ts, and Always-Haves

Most of us don't often sit around and think about all the ways we are messing up our lives. In fact, we try pretty hard not to think about them. Even for people who do get bummed out fairly often, it's common to spend that time wanting the world or other people to change. And when we do turn our attention to what *we* could do that might help to move us toward lives we value, we tend to admonish ourselves pretty fiercely.

Even though we try not to dwell there, most of us know exactly what we're doing that's not working in our lives, along with what we are not doing that would make things better. We could give you a list of every domain of human living and you could tell us something you should or shouldn't be doing. You should eat more vegetables. You shouldn't drive faster than the speed limit. You should call your grandmother more often. You shouldn't gossip about the not-so-friendly girl you work with. You could fill a few pages with shoulds and shouldn'ts, and actually, you're probably right on. Choosing to change all that stuff probably would make your life better. Somehow, though, knowing you should do something isn't enough to make you choose it. And frankly, doing it without choosing it doesn't seem to work too well either.

See, there are times when your shoulds sort of work. You think, *I should call my grandmother.* You ignore it the first time, and each subsequent time, but finally it gets to be too much. So you clench your teeth and take a deep breath, and you dial her up. Not because you love the woman (even though you really do), not because you want to connect with her (even though you'd be sad if you couldn't), but because it feels like you have to. And as you sit there alternating between listening to her describe her ailments and answering mechanically when she asks how you're doing in school and work, you miss the love and connection that are there to be had.

And for the times when the shoulds don't work, it's usually because they're not showing up alone. They've got some big can't that follows up right behind them. Often our can'ts are the ones that point out some practical obstacle in the world. *I should do more volunteer work, but I can't—I don't have time. I should recycle, but I can't—there's no curbside pickup. I should talk to my boss about that project, but I can't—she doesn't listen.* The most problematic ones are often the can'ts about us. *I shouldn't smoke cigarettes, but I can't quit—I have no willpower. I should take care of things ahead of time, but I can't—I'm lazy.*

Sometimes it's not a can't that comes along, it's an always-have. Sometimes, we don't even bother to come up with a good reason why we do the things we do and don't do the things we don't. We just do. Always have. So we do. We just don't. Never have. So we don't. We keep doing it like we've always done it, and we don't want to risk trying something different.

If all this sounds familiar, it should. We've already discussed the things that keep us stuck in our lives. It's not the shoulds, have-to's, can'ts, or always-haves that show up that are the problem. It's our inflexibility when they show up. They show up and we lose contact with the present. They show up and we fuse with them, seeing ourselves and the world and others through them. They show up and we start doing whatever we can to avoid being touched by them, moved by them. They show up and we lose ourselves behind what we should be, always have been, and can't ever be.

Until recently, that is. Recently you started practicing something different. Recently you started taking the same old stuff that gets you stuck and calling it up with purpose and intention. You've noticed the times when your awareness is scattered or stuck, and you've practiced being present and aware. You've noticed the times when you are seeing the world through your thoughts, and you've practiced defusing and letting the rest of the world fill in. You've noticed when you are in run-trap-kill mode in your own life, and you've practiced accepting your experiences as they unfold. You've noticed when you are seeing yourself and others through your thoughts, and you've practiced getting to know you and others as more than whatever your mind is offering in that moment.

And you've done all this with experiences that really seem to shut you out of your life. You've practiced flexibility with your body image. And you've come back to this practice over and over. There were moments when you set this job down, when you turned away from this piece of work, but if you made it this far, that means you always turned back. In the flexibility model, that turning back is what commitment is about. It's not the promise that matters, and it's not that the promise controls your behavior for all time. What matters is that you come back on to the job, one more time than you find yourself away.

Pause now and call to mind the journey you've taken. See if you can't reach back in your mind to before you started this piece of work. Notice the thoughts and feelings you carried *and* the way you carried them. Call to mind what it was like for you when you first cracked this book open. What kind of impressions did you have? What kind of experiences came up for you and what did you do with them?

Notice what has changed. Notice what hasn't changed a bit. And with your changed stuff and your not-so-changed stuff gathered up where you can really feel it and get it, take a moment to acknowledge the work that you've done.

So what now? If you're not careful, you could finish up this book today, look out at your life, and find yourself wrapping everything you've practiced back into more shoulds and have-to's. You could make being flexible another place you have to measure up. You could make the values you've chosen just more rules to follow to be enough. And the hurt and failure you feel around your body could grow with the hurt and failure you would feel around not pulling this flexibility thing off. You could dig your heels in and find a way you do what you've always done.

You could. You get to pick. But then, you'd always wonder if you hadn't caught a glimpse once of something different, if there wasn't another chance somewhere you could offer yourself. And, of course, you'd be right to wonder, because even if your changes have been small, you've got your hands on something different right now.

An Alternative: Seeing and Taking Opportunities for Change

When we first invited you along on this journey, we mentioned four opportunities for change:

- *Being present,* or noticing your ongoing experiences of your body and the world as they occur in and around you

- *Seeing beyond your thoughts,* or noticing your thoughts about your body without letting them dominate your experience

- *Accepting experience,* or opening up to those dominating thoughts and the feelings that come with them

- *Getting to know you,* or contacting the you that is more than the way you see, feel, and think about your body

Then we went one by one through each of these opportunities, offering explanations of them and invitations to experience your own flexibilities and inflexibilities in each domain. Then came the most important part: at the end of each chapter, we invited you to look for these opportunities out in your world. We asked you to notice where and when you were fused, or not present, or avoidant, or acting out some story about yourself. Then we invited you to do something different.

Take a few moments now to look over some of the commitments you've made to notice inflexibility and build flexibility. Call to mind those commitments that brought you closer to the things that really matter to you, closer to your values.

The challenge we bring to you now is no different, really. Recognize inflexibility in your life, not as a story about your struggle up in your head, but in the moment that you are being inflexible. And build flexibility. One moment at a time. Not as a have-to, but as a choice. Not to fix what's broken, but to appreciate what just is and what could be. If you're following along with the audio files, please turn to track 17.

PRACTICE: Values Compass

Give yourself three slow, full breaths and let your eyes fall gently closed. And breathe, taking a moment to notice what it feels like to take air into your body and to release it.

And with your next breath, see if you can't call to mind the experiences you've had in the weeks you've spent working through this book. Let it be that you create right now, with just your breath, a place where your memories of the journey you've taken could unfold. From the hardest moments to the easiest, from the most stuck to the freest. From the moments you were farthest from the person you want to be to the moments you settled in and just were. And breathe.

And see if you can't simply observe for a moment—watching the memories unfold and tumble past, all out of order, some fuzzy or with gaps. Notice the way some tug at you, or stir some feeling up, if only for a moment. And breathe.

And see if you can't, with your breath, stretch the walls of your awareness out, to where you can call up these memories with more and more breadth and depth, to where they can pass through you gently, to where you can feel each of them passing through you. And breathe.

And on your next breath, notice the you that holds all these memories, the you that can call them up now, and the you that can notice you. Let it be that with each breath you are more and more aware of your own perspectives on these memories as they unfold in the now, and on the thoughts and feelings that come with them. And breathe.

And now, see if you can't, from the jumble of memories, let certain glimpses, certain moments of your life in the past few weeks rise up beyond the others. Let yourself notice the moments of sweetness, the moments when you set down your struggle with body image and let yourself sink into your skin, even if there was hard stuff around and inside. A moment when you were free in your own body and filled with some bit of sweetness that you've known. And breathe.

See that moment that rises up clearly before you, like you were watching it on a trailer about your life. Notice where you were, and who, if anyone, was there with you. Notice what you were doing, how you held yourself there. Notice the expression on your face. See if you can't let more and more details fill in with each breath. And breathe.

And when you've got that sweet spot clearly before you, let it be that you were suddenly aware of a compass in your hand with a single button. Take a moment to feel its weight there, and feel the button under your thumb. And breathe.

And on your next breath, imagine that you could breathe yourself into that sweet spot in your life. That you could pour your consciousness into you in that moment, seeing the world through your eyes in that moment. And breathe, letting the sweetness fill you right now from the tips of your toes to the top of your head, and noticing the sadness that is so often blended right in with the sweet. And breathe.

And when you feel yourself filled with the sad and the sweet of what it means to be free in your body in your life, give the button on your compass a squeeze, marking the values present here in this moment, setting the compass to remember and point the way. And breathe.

And on your next breath, let rise up another moment of sweetness you've encountered on your journey, maybe from another domain of your life in which you've found freedom and vitality, if even for a moment. And breathe.

Again, let that sweet moment unfold before you, noticing where you were, what you were doing, how you held yourself. And breathe.

And when the scene is clear before you, give yourself a slow, full breath and breathe yourself into your skin in that moment, letting the sweetness fill you up more and more with each breath. See the world through your eyes in that sweet moment, and notice what it feels like to set down your struggle with body image, to be free in your own body, in your own life. See if you can't make room for the sadness tangled right in with the sweetness you carry. And breathe.

And when you feel yourself filled with the sad and the sweet of what it means to be free in your body in your life, squeeze the button on your compass, marking the values present here, setting the compass to remember and point the way. And breathe.

And on your next breath, let rise up another moment of sweetness you've encountered on your journey, from yet another domain of your life in which you've found freedom. And breathe.

Once more, let this sweet moment become more and more real as you breathe, remembering the details of where you were, what you were doing, and how you held yourself. And breathe.

And when you've got a clear picture of a moment of sweetness you've known, see if you can't breathe yourself into that sweet moment, and feel it fill you right now.

And when you feel yourself filled with the sad and the sweet of what it means to be free in your body in your life, squeeze the button on your compass, marking the values present here, setting the compass to remember and point the way. And breathe.

And on your next breath, let that scene fade from you, the memories gently falling away as you breathe yourself back into this moment right now, but still outside yourself, with our little book in front of you. And even as you find yourself back in your skin in this moment, let it be that you can still feel the weight of the compass you've set in your hand. Watch you here for a moment, eyes closed and breathing. As you feel the air enter your body, watch your chest and belly rise before you. And breathe.

And imagine that you could make of this compass a gift, that you could approach yourself right now and offer it—a way to find your way back to the life you care about, to the things most precious to you.

And whenever you're ready, breathe yourself back into your skin in this moment. Give yourself three slow, full breaths, then let your eyes come open.

Take a moment now to make a few notes as to where your values compass would point you, what your valued life includes. Don't limit yourself to the domains you touched on in the exercise.

Who would you be in the moments in which you were heading toward your most meaningful life? Who would you be in your relationships? In your work? How would you grow and push yourself to develop? How would you care for your body? For your spirit? How would you serve your community? Who would you be in the world? You might even sketch a small compass with "north" pointing to a few words that represent, for you, your values.

What if navigating the most challenging moments in your life is as simple as opening up to what is available in this moment and looking for a point of connection with the things that matter to you? Noticing the shoulds, the can'ts, the have-to's and always-haves, and choosing a direction you could step that puts you a bit closer to the you that you want to be? What if that is how flexibility is built—one step at a time, one hard moment at a time? What if stringing those valued steps together, one after another, is really all a valued life is?

Challenge and Commitment: When the World Doesn't Cooperate

Of course, just because something is simple doesn't mean that it's easy. You've been struggling with your body for a long time. It's where you've lived and what you know. And that struggle didn't come out of nowhere. You learned to struggle with your body, even when it meant letting go of what you care about. And just because you've been growing and changing doesn't mean your world has. In fact, as you've begun to do things differently, you've probably noticed the world pushing back. It's worth thinking about the contexts that support body image inflexibility for you, along with how you might 1) change those contexts to keep yourself moving in a valued direction or 2) change your relationship with those contexts.

The Big World: Society We Live In

For one, much of the world at large is pretty willing to adopt the idea that physical attractiveness is important, objective, and easy to change. For many, it feels like we have a responsibility to society to be attractive. Why wouldn't you make the extra effort to make yourself pleasant to look at? And it's not just about others. Everywhere you go, you receive messages about the way that you *should* look and what you might risk missing out on if you don't. Your broad shoulders will make people listen to you. Your full lips will attract a lover. Your big breasts will make you happy. Your thick hair will make you confident. Your smooth skin will make you nicer. Your button nose will help you have more fun. And it's not just about getting things you don't have, it's about getting rid of things you do. Everywhere you go, you're exposed to the million-dollar idea that looking a particular way might finally bring relief from all your struggles.

Take a moment to jot down the kinds of messages to which you're most susceptible, where you run into these, and when they tend to influence you the most. And now, notice which of these messages show up with values attached, and which of them just don't.

For example, you might notice that some of the magazines you read or television shows you watch do more to keep you stuck than to help you move toward anything you value. It may be that another magazine or TV show would do just as well to keep you entertained without making your world harder than it needs to be.

On the other hand, it may be that the career or hobby you love involves attention to the body and pushes body image inflexibility for you, but that there's still something you care about of which you wouldn't want to let go. For example, if you love to dance or your work as a news anchor, turning away from these would mean turning away from the life you want. This is tough because you end up hurting yourself *and* losing the very thing you value. In this case, the challenge would be to practice noticing the moments in which inflexibility takes over, and practice shifting back to your values *in that challenging context itself*. If this applies to you, we invite you to repeat some of the practices you got the most out of, either with experiences specific to that situation, or in the situation itself.

The Small World: Folks We Love

It's not just a big, bad society that doesn't support body image flexibility. Individuals in our personal lives often struggle to support us when we're making big changes. Just as part of who you are is who you are to others, part of who your loved ones are is who they are to you. So when you start changing, the relationship will have to change if it is going to survive. You'll probably find that the folks in your life are not any more flexible than you were when you first got this book. You might suddenly notice what they are fused with and how they avoid things. Some of the folks in your life probably struggle with body image as much as you have. In fact, some of your relationships probably have your body image struggles all tangled up inside them. There are certain things those who love you have learned to do when your struggles (and their struggles) get bad. Some of those work well and keep you moving toward your values. Others are in direct contrast to what you've been trying to do here, but will still be hard to let go of. Finally, some folks in your life won't share your values. They just won't get what you're about. In all of these cases, you might feel judged or abandoned. Or you might find yourself judging and abandoning.

Take a moment to jot down the relationships in your life that are most important, and how they affect your striving for body image flexibility toward your valued life. And now notice the values that are at stake in each of these relationships.

Of course, some of these relationships will not hold much value for you. You'll decide that your continued progress toward a valued life is more important to you than keeping a friendship with someone who doesn't support you and your flexibility. It's not, however, always easy to tell ahead of time how folks will interact with this kind of hard stuff. After all, your friends and family, just like you, have struggled their fair share, and probably haven't thought much about alternatives. For the relationships that you really care about investing in, it may be worth talking in a really specific way about what you are trying to do and what kind of support you want. Your loved ones don't have to work the whole book to be able to get that you are trying something different and that you want them to help you do things differently. Just be sure that you approach this talk in terms of what you want to share, not what you are expecting to get. If it's only going to feel valuable if you get a certain response, it might be best to hold off.

The Inside World: The Stuff We Carry

Finally, there are, most likely, thoughts and feelings pushing you around that you haven't come close to drawing out and working on with the flexibility model. Some of these you haven't really touched because they don't seem to be part of your struggles with body image. Maybe you're constantly fighting off anxiety. Maybe you struggle with being smart enough or nice enough or strong enough. Maybe you carry hard memories that you've never been able to fully shake.

Some of these you haven't worked on because they are not really part of your day-to-day experience. Often the thoughts and feelings and memories we carry have layers, from the easiest to deal with (like feeling annoyed with someone) to the most difficult to deal with (like feeling abandoned by a parent). Sometimes we are so inflexible with an experience that we're not even clear on what exactly is showing up there. You may have already noticed that when you open up to and defuse from a thought or feeling, you often experience life in a clearer, but deeper and more painful way. Throughout this journey, you've done a ton of work on lots of different kinds of experiences. And there are likely still experiences you've yet to open up to that are keeping you from living your most valued life. The flexibility model is not just about body image. It can be applied to all difficult experiences.

Take a moment to jot down experiences you have that you'd like to become more flexible with but that you haven't done much work on. Then notice if there are experiences that you know get you stuck, but you don't see yourself ever working on. You might take a moment to wonder whether you might find some worth in building flexibility around those experiences, not as a have-to, but as a choice.

Valued Commitment: Stepping Forward, Turning Back

We've ended every chapter of this book by having you think about what you value and notice how some aspect of inflexibility has interfered with you moving forward toward that value. Then we've had you make a series of three small commitments. Now, as we reach the end of our final chapter, we're bringing you the same challenge. Except this time, instead of your commitments being small moves that stretch out over a week, we're going to ask you to look a little deeper, to stretch a little more. Take a full breath and find a fresh page to work on. Write the numbers 1 through 3 with a few blank lines after every number.

First, consider the things you might experience and choices you might make over the next month. And ask yourself: If you were to bring what you've learned about flexibility out into your life and use it to continue to return, over and over for the next month, to the you that you want to be, what would be evident? What would you see as you looked back? What would be apparent to others? Now choose just one aspect of what you see emerging over the next month—one relationship, one situation, one domain of your life—and consider a commitment you might make to carry out that change. Be specific about what it is you do now, what the impact of that is, what you'll do to move toward your values, and what other opportunities for change might help that happen. The more specific your commitment, the more likely it will be that you'll give it a shot. Take your time, using your notes and past practices for guidance. When you have chosen a commitment, take a moment to write it down next to number 1. Choose a date about one month from now as the date for carrying out this commitment, and write it down.

For your second commitment, let yourself imagine a few months have passed, and you've been building your flexibility and moving steadily toward the life you care about. Let it be that you've found yourself struggling more than once, sometimes terribly, but that you've always found your way back. As you looked back on the three or four months that had passed, what would you see you had changed? What would be apparent to others? Now choose just one aspect of what you see emerging over the next three or four months and consider a commitment you might make to carry out that change. Again, be specific about what it is you do now, what the impact of that is, what you'll do to move toward your values, and what other opportunities for change might help that happen. When you have chosen a commitment, take a moment to write it down next to number 2. Write a date down that is three or four months from now as the date you'll carry out this commitment by.

For your final commitment, let your mind reach out into wondering what you might accomplish over the next year. After twelve months, you'd likely have encountered a number of struggles, some of which took you out of your valued life for a long time. Yet, let it be that each time, you found your way back to the things you care about and set back to your valued path. On the other side of a year, what might be different about how you were living? Twelve months after you started striving for flexibility, what shifts might you see in your life? Approach this final commitment gently, choosing some aspect of what you see emerging over the next year to commit yourself to. Remember to be specific about what it is you do now, what the impact of that is, what you'll do to move toward your values, and what other opportunities for change might help that happen.

When you've got your commitments recorded, let your eyes fall closed and give yourself a slow, deep breath. Here you are, in that scary, but by now familiar place, where you've just put a commitment out into the world. Notice not only how difficult commitment is, but also see if you aren't holding that difficulty differently. Notice if it isn't the case that you are getting better and better at committing all the time. You might wonder: What if this is it? What if choosing, committing, and coming back to the things you care about is what it's all about?

8 Reaching Out: Making Use of Other Resources

As you move out into your year, then the rest of your life, you might find yourself looking for ways to connect back up with this kind of work. It can be hard to transition from consistent reading and commitments to seeing when a certain practice or commitment is in order. We don't think there's any reason you couldn't pick this book back up at any point and work through it with a fresh notebook and your favorite pen. We feel like you could do the same sit fifty times, and you'd experience it differently each and every time, so you might just save the audio files of the practices somewhere handy and come back to those here and there.

Other Texts

If you've taken to the psychological flexibility model and feel you've benefited from the structure of the practices we offered in this book, you might want to pick up another acceptance and commitment therapy workbook. Every book describes the ACT perspective a little differently, and each includes different ways of practicing psychological flexibility. It may be that things you are still a bit fuzzy on would clear up completely with a different example, metaphor, or exercise.

Steven C. Hayes's workbook with Spencer Smith, *Get Out of Your Mind and Into Your Life: The New Acceptance and Commitment Therapy* (2005), offers an introduction to ACT that doesn't focus on any one kind of diagnosis or problem. Kelly G. Wilson's book with Troy, *Things Might Go Terribly, Horribly Wrong* (2010), focuses on anxiety, which often comes along with body image difficulties. If your body image struggles are related to eating problems, our book with Kelly, *The Mindfulness and Acceptance Workbook for Bulimia* (2011) might be helpful. If your difficulties are related more to self-starvation and being underweight, Michelle Heffner and Georg H. Eifert wrote *The Anorexia Workbook: How to Accept Yourself, Heal Your Suffering, and Reclaim Your Life* (2004).

If your interest in ACT moves from practical to intellectual, there is also a book on ACT for body image that is available for professionals. Adria Pearson, Michelle Heffner, and Victoria Follette published a therapist's manual, *Acceptance and Commitment Therapy for Body Image Dissatisfaction* (2010), which focuses on how to treat body image struggles from an ACT perspective. It's quite a bit more technical than this one, digging deeply into the theory and basic behavioral science that underlies this work. If you find yourself intrigued by the ACT perspective, however, it may be worth taking a look.

Connecting with the ACT Community

If you're not quite ready to leap into more reading, you might just pay a visit to the website for the Association for Contextual Behavior Science, or ACBS. Unlike most professional association websites, ACBS maintains all kinds of different resources for folks who aren't professionals. A good place to start is the "ACT for the Public" page at contextualscience.org/act_for_the_public. This page offers links to more self-help resources, information about the theory and research behind ACT, ACT-relevant articles, videos, and interviews. It also offers directions on how to join the e-mail listserv. Many find it appealing to connect with other individuals who are trying on the flexibility model and looking for some support. Finally, it offers tips on how to find an ACT therapist. It may be that your work with us has opened you up to the possibilities of what you could do with more intensive therapeutic support. Of course, you'll always get the most out of therapy if you're approaching it as something you're choosing rather than something it seems you have to do.

Conclusion

A Final Invitation

And this is the part where we leave you to the rest of your journey. We can't be sure where all you've been or what all you've seen there, and we definitely can't possibly know what's next for you. We do, however, get to hope. We started this book with a hope. We started with a hope so crazy that we abandoned the book three or four times before we could fully choose to write it. The struggle seemed too big, too universal for our little voices to make any difference. And yet, in finally choosing to write the book, the hope we started with has only grown.

We are so grateful to have had the opportunity to offer you this little journey. And we hope that from here on out, on more days than not, you might greet your body (and the hate that comes with it) with appreciation for what it feels like to be human in your body today, then to freely step out into the life that matters to you.

We invite you to hope the same.

References

Armatas, C., D. Holt, and M. Rice. 2003. "Impacts of an Online-Supported, Resource-Based Learning Environment: Does One Size Fit All?" *Distance Education* 24(2): 141-158.

Bach, P., and S. C. Hayes. 2002. "The Use of Acceptance and Commitment Therapy to Prevent the Rehospitalization of Psychotic Patients: A Randomized Controlled Trial." *Journal of Consulting and Clinical Psychology* 70(5): 1129-1139.

Brown, L. A., E. M. Forman, J. D. Herbert, K. L. Hoffman, E. K. Yuen, and E. M. Goetter. 2011. "A Randomized Controlled Trial of Acceptance-Based Behavior Therapy and Cognitive Therapy for Test Anxiety: A Pilot Study." *Behavior Modification* 35(1): 31-53. doi: 10.1177/0145445510390930.

Cash, T. 2008. *The Body Image Workbook*. Oakland, CA: New Harbinger Publications.

Cohen, S., B. Gottlieb, and L. Underwood. 2000. "Social Relationships and Health." In *Social Support Measurement and Intervention*, edited by Sheldon Cohen, Lynn Underwood, and Benjamin Gottlieb. New York: Oxford University Press.

Crow, S., M. Eisenberg, M. Story, and D. Neumark-Sztainer. 2008. "Suicidal Behavior in Adolescents: Relationship to Weight Status, Weight Control Behaviors, and Body Dissatisfaction." *International Journal of Eating Disorders* 41(1): 82–87.

Downs, D., J. DiNallo, and T. Kirner. 2008. "Determinants of Pregnancy and Postpartum Depression: Prospective Influences of Depressive Symptoms, Body Image Satisfaction, and Exercise Behavior." *Annals of Behavioral Medicine* 36(1): 54–63.

Eifert, G. H., J. P. Forsyth, J. Arch, E. Espejo, M. Keller, and D. Langer. 2009. "Acceptance and Commitment Therapy for Anxiety Disorders: Three Case Studies Exemplifying a Unified Treatment Protocol." *Cognitive and Behavioral Practice* 16(4): 368-385.

England, E. L., J. D. Herbert, E. M. Forman, S. J. Rabin, A. Juarascio, and S. P. Goldstein. 2012. "Acceptance-Based Exposure Therapy for Public Speaking Anxiety." *Journal of Contextual Behavioral Science* 1(1-2): 66-72.

Forrest, K., and W. Stuhldreher. 2007. "Patterns and Correlates of Body Image Dissatisfaction and Distortion Among College Students." *American Journal of Health Studies* 22(1): 18-25.

Gaudiano, B. A., and J. D. Herbert. 2006. "Believability of Hallucinations as a Potential Mediator of Their Frequency and Associated Distress in Psychotic Inpatients." *Behavioural and Cognitive Psychotherapy* 34(4): 497–502.

Grant J., L. Levine, D. Kim, and M. N. Potenza. 2005. "Impulse Control Disorders in Adult Psychiatric Inpatients." *American Journal of Psychiatry* 162(11): 2184–2188.

Gregg, J. A., G. M. Callaghan, S. C. Hayes, and J. L. Glenn-Lawson. 2007. "Improving Diabetes Self-Management Through Acceptance, Mindfulness, and Values: A Randomized Controlled Trial." *Journal of Consulting and Clinical Psychology* 75(2): 336-343.

Hayes, S. C., J. Luoma, F. Bond, A. Masuda, and J. Lillis. 2006. "Acceptance and Commitment Therapy: Model, Processes, and Outcomes." *Behaviour Research and Therapy* 44(1): 1-25.

Hayes, S. C., K. Strosahl, and K. G. Wilson. 1999. *Acceptance and Commitment Therapy: An Experiential Approach to Behavior Change.* New York: Guilford Press.

Kashdan, T. B., and J. Rottenberg. 2010. "Psychological Flexibility as a Fundamental Aspect of Health." *Clinical Psychology Review* 30(7): 865-878.

Leary, M., and R. Kowalski. 1995. *Social Anxiety.* New York: Guilford Press.

Lundgren, T., J. Dahl, L. Melin, and B. Kies. 2006. "Evaluation of Acceptance and Commitment Therapy for Drug Refractory Epilepsy: A Randomized Controlled Trial in South Africa—A Pilot Study." *Epilepsia* 47(12): 2173–2179.

McCracken, L. M., K. E. Vowles, and C. Eccleston. 2004. "Acceptance of Chronic Pain: Component Analysis and a Revised Assessment Method." *Pain* 107(1-2): 159-66.

Moran, D. J. 2011. "ACT for Leadership: Using Acceptance and Commitment Training to Develop Crisis-Resilient Change Managers." *International Journal of Behavioral Consultation and Therapy* 7(1): 68-77.

Muennig, P., H. Jia, R. Lee, and E. Lubetkin. 2008. "Do Psychosocial Health Risks Explain the Relationship Between Body Mass Index and Health?" *American Journal of Public Health* 98: 501-506.

Peterson, B. D., G. H. Eifert, T. Feingold, and S. Davidson. 2009. "Using Acceptance and Commitment Therapy (ACT) to Treat Distressed Couples: A Case Study with Two Couples." *Cognitive and Behavioral Practice* 16(4): 430-442.

Phillips, K., and D. Castle. 2002. "Body Dysmorphic Disorder." In *Disorders of Body Image,* edited by D. Castle and K. Phillips. London: Wrightson Biomedical.

Phillips, K., M. Coles, W. Menard, S. Yen, C. Fay, and R. Weisberg. 2005. "Suicidal Ideation and Suicide Attempts in Body Dysmorphic Disorder." *Journal of Clinical Psychiatry* 66(6): 717–725.

Stice, E., R. Cameron, J. Killen, C. Hayward, and C. Taylor. 2000. "Body-Image and Eating Disturbances Predict Onset of Depression Among Female Adolescents: A Longitudinal Study." *Journal of Abnormal Psychology* 109(3): 438-444.

Vickers, K., C. Patten, C. Bronars, K. Lane, S. Stevens, I. Croghan, D. Schroeder, and M. Clark. 2004. "Binge Drinking in Female College Students: The Association of Physical Activity, Weight Concern, and Depressive Symptoms." *Journal of American College Health* 53(3): 133–140.

Zettle, R. D., and J. C. Rains. 1989. "Group Cognitive and Contextual Therapies in Treatment of Depression." *Journal of Clinical Psychology* 45(3): 436-445.

Zettle, R. D., and S. C. Hayes. 1986. "Dysfunctional Control by Client Verbal Behavior: The Context of Reason Giving." *The Analysis of Verbal Behavior* 4: 30-38.

Emily K. Sandoz, PhD, is assistant professor of psychology at University of Louisiana at Lafayette, LA. She is a therapist who specializes in treating clients using acceptance and commitment therapy. Sandoz is coauthor of *Acceptance and Commitment Therapy for Eating Disorders* and *Mindfulness and Acceptance for Bulimia*. She received her doctorate from the University of Mississippi, and she lives and works in Lafayette, LA.

Troy DuFrene is a writer in the San Francisco Bay Area who specializes in psychology. He is coauthor of *Coping with OCD; Mindfulness for Two; Things Might Go Terribly, Horribly Wrong; Acceptance and Commitment Therapy for Eating Disorders;* and *Mindfulness and Acceptance for Bulimia*.

Register your **new harbinger** titles for additional benefits!

When you register your **new harbinger** title—purchased in any format, from any source—you get access to benefits like the following:

- Downloadable accessories like printable worksheets and extra content

- Instructional videos and audio files

- Information about updates, corrections, and new editions

Not every title has accessories, but we're adding new material all the time.

Access free accessories in 3 easy steps:

1. Sign in at NewHarbinger.com (or **register** to create an account).

2. Click on **register a book**. Search for your title and click the **register** button when it appears.

3. Click on the **book cover or title** to go to its details page. Click on **accessories** to view and access files.

That's all there is to it!

If you need help, visit:

NewHarbinger.com/accessories

new harbinger
CELEBRATING
40 YEARS

FROM OUR PUBLISHER—

As the publisher at New Harbinger and a clinical psychologist since 1978, I know that emotional problems are best helped with evidence-based therapies. These are the treatments derived from scientific research (randomized controlled trials) that show what works. Whether these treatments are delivered by trained clinicians or found in a self-help book, they are designed to provide you with proven strategies to overcome your problem.

Therapies that aren't evidence-based—whether offered by clinicians or in books—are much less likely to help. In fact, therapies that aren't guided by science may not help you at all. That's why this New Harbinger book is based on scientific evidence that the treatment can relieve emotional pain.

This is important: if this book isn't enough, and you need the help of a skilled therapist, use the following resource to find a clinician trained in the evidence-based protocols appropriate for your problem.

Real help is available for the problems you have been struggling with. The skills you can learn from evidence-based therapies will change your life.

Matthew McKay, PhD
Publisher, New Harbinger Publications

new harbinger
CELEBRATING
40 YEARS

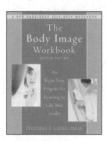